TELL-TALE
TEXAS

T0275012

TELL-TALE
TEXAS

Investigations in
Infamous History

E.R. BILLS

Foreword by
Robin Wells

THE
History
PRESS

Published by The History Press
Charleston, SC
www.historypress.com

Front cover, clockwise from top left: public domain; courtesy of *Fort Worth Star-Telegram*; photo by author; photo by Dorothy Redus Robinson; public domain; dynamite: Wikimedia Commons.
Back cover, top left: courtesy of DeGolyer Library, Southern Methodist University; *top right*: public domain; gun: Wikimedia Commons.

First published 2023

Manufactured in the United States

ISBN 9781467154345

Library of Congress Control Number: 2023934783

Notice: The information in this book is true and complete to the best of our knowledge. It is offered without guarantee on the part of the author or The History Press. The author and The History Press disclaim all liability in connection with the use of this book.

History is heavily edited for school-children and, for most of us, commencement puts an end to study. Thus we go through life with notions of our past which, for depth, complexity, subtlety of shading, rank with comic books. Texas history particularly lends itself to this; it is so farfetched that only a child would believe it.

—William Humphrey, *No Resting Place*

For my mother and father

CONTENTS

FOREWORD

Who do you get when you cross the anti-lynching campaigner Ida B. Wells and gimlet-eyed social observer Hunter S. Thompson? I would like to nominate E.R. Bills. And it is more than apt that he is a product of the mighty state of Texas. Bills says the quiet parts out loud. Very loud, indeed, in an irreverent, scornful and heartfelt way that is his version of being plainspoken in Texas.

I first came across Bills's work when doing some research on my family's East Texas roots. Having fled Texas at the age of sixteen for college and never looking back, I studiously avoided the topic for decades. Like my maternal great-grandparents, who moved from the Houston County farming towns of Lovelady and Crockett to the "big city" of Dallas in 1910, I looked forward. As the old Negro spiritual says, "Can't plow straight an' keep-a looking back."

Yet.

As we grow older and wiser, we come to learn that there is always a "yet." There comes a time to look back. And as you will learn from reading *Tell-Tale Texas*, as well as Bills's previous works—*The 1910 Slocum Massacre: An Act of Genocide in East Texas, Black Holocaust: The Paris Horror and the Legacy of Texas Terror*, other historical examinations and assorted editorials—Bills delivers the goods on Texas. Stripping away the literal whitewashing of the state's history, he recounts the brutal and shocking facts of the "lost" (as in "purposely lost") history of the Lone Star State. On a personal level, Bills's work revealed to me why so many of us fled—some of us physically fleeing, others fleeing in their minds—the terrors and ghosts of our collective Texan past.

The chapters in *Tell-Tale Texas* cover events from a variety of periods. Among these events are the 1976 assassination of a Black civil rights leader, the legalized murder of an Indigenous American sex worker in 2009, the 1919 burning at the stake of a mentally disabled Black man by a white mob, the effective 1940s book burning of the Fort Worth memoir *The Inheritors*, the 1857 terror campaign by whites against Mexican American drovers and the unaddressed epidemic of murders and suicides of the war-traumatized soldiers stationed at Fort Hood.

One could ask what ties these events together as a picture of the great state of Texas? What is Bills saying about the nature of the Texas collective? To my Dallas-bred eye, what Bills's work makes clear is that, in Texas, impunity goes hand in hand with suppression. And suppression takes many forms: a coroner's report, book banning, jurisprudence nullified by ethnic homogeneity or simply collective silencing and myth-making. Suppression delivered with a southern smile, but also with an unmistakable air of menace, often with a lynching rope handy.

Now that the Texas penchant for historical erasure has been adopted as a national strategy of the Trumpist Republican right—aka the attack on their bogeymen of "woke-ism" and "critical race theory"—it is more important than ever that we recognize writers like E.R. Bills, writers who take a stand against the erasure of inconvenient history. Bills is alerting us to the Faulknerian truth that not only is the past not past, but also that the mythologization of the past is political in twenty-first century America, just as it has been for over 150 years in Texas.

The attacks by the right on an honest and unflinching appraisal of this country's often wishful memory are clearly a form of retaliation for daring to speak historical accuracy to power. Bills is part of the lineage of authors who have investigated and memorialized the massacres of Black people in Tulsa, Oklahoma; Rosewood, Florida; Elaine, Arkansas; and Wilmington, North Carolina. Doubtless, there are many more American horrors to be rediscovered. These writers are the vanguard in the battle to drag this country out of its hypocrisy, selective amnesia and addiction to violence. The deeper the historical dissociation, the deeper the rage when the disassociation is pointed out. Thus Donald Trump is the logical endpoint of the whitewashing of American history. Can it be a coincidence that Trump kicked off his second presidential run in Waco, Texas, with an apocalyptic speech promising violence and retribution? On the thirtieth anniversary of the Branch Davidian battle, no less?

Reader, treat this book reverently. It is an act of sleuthing, an act of commitment to the forgotten victims, an act of fortitude in facing the unspeakable, an act of demythologizing the roots of Texan white male supremacy. And above all, it is an act of moral courage.

—Robin Wells, PhD
Born at Parkland Hospital, Dallas, Texas, 1959

ACKNOWLEDGEMENTS

Special thanks to David Martin Davies, Constance Hollie-Jawaid, Robin Wells, Norris White, Rodney A. Howard, Leigh Craven, Barbara Wooten, Steven A. Reich, Debbie Hiott, Ben Gibson, Christen Thompson, Billy Huckaby and too many others to name.

INTRODUCTION

They say the victors write the history, but here in Texas, this dictum is only partially true. We also "white" the history, forgetting the diversity that ensured our victories.

It leaves wagonloads of unfinished business, and maybe more unfinished than finished, especially in terms of culture and heritage. Sometimes, when you confront the past, the past confronts you back.

I was not entirely unaware of this, even in high school. But shortly into my university studies, the scale and breadth of our historical unawareness and utter obliviousness—in Texas and across America—shocked me. And I don't think I ever completely recovered.

Where is the intelligentsia on the great, gaping chasms that stare accusingly from our textbooks? Where are our fine, sturdily endowed public and private universities? Where are our thinkers? Where are our formerly trademark contrarians?

The thing is, nobody in particular—academic, historian or present-day journo—has to dig real deep to uncover cracks in the state's proverbial façade. Especially now. That's why we are where we are. That's why historical amnesia is an unspoken directive. That's why white fragility is king. That's why everything isn't really bigger in Texas, and, in truth, so many things are just plain small.

This is not a book I intended to write. This is not a book that will please many of my neighbors or appease the victims of historic neglect. This is not a book that will be nominated for the usual awards. This is not a book that will appear in many school libraries. This is not a book many Texans will appreciate. But that, of course, is why it needed to be written.

We should no longer avert our eyes to what went on. This is who we were and, in some sense, still are. Our ignorance is indefensible and asinine in ways that should never stop offending us.

—E.R. Bills
March 31, 2023

1

THE ASSASSINATION OF FRANK J. ROBINSON

Demoralize the enemy from within by surprise, terror, sabotage, assassination.
This is the war of the future.
—Adolf Hitler

We exchanged sideways glances. It was a dubious claim, and the former judge we were talking to followed it with a glaring non sequitur.

"I think he killed himself," insisted seventy-six-year-old Alexander Nemer. "I mean, look at the photos. Part of the man's head is missing. Something blew it off. There's a picture of a cat licking the inside of his skull when he's there on the garage floor. I would generally say something took the top of his head off."

Ignoring the disturbing image this statement conjured, Texas Public Radio reporter David Martin Davies and I pointed out that that was why we were there. The crime scene photos, autopsy files, police records and the inquest documents were all gone, vanished, and no one—including myself and Davies—could find them.

Nemer simply informed us that he had given the inquest files to the court clerk when the hearing was concluded.

Davies pressed on, asking Nemer if the photo in question actually proved that the victim shot himself or that he was shot, possibly by someone else. I reminded Nemer that Texas Ranger Bob Prince had testified at the inquest and said there was no gunpowder residue on the victim's body. We asked Nemer how that was possible.

"I'm not here to speculate," Nemer said. "I'm only here to tell you what happened."[1]

The official details of the crime, so far as they exist, are limited to a report issued by the Texas Department of Public Safety (DPS), dated Oct. 15, 1976: County, *Anderson*; Place of Occurrence, *Palestine*; Victim, *Frank J. Robinson*; Offense, *Questionable Death*.

Outside of the contemporary newspaper coverage, the DPS report on this seventy-four-year-old Black man's death is all that's left. Everything else is missing.

The initial DPS findings, filed by Prince, an officer of Company F of the Texas Rangers, is twelve pages long and communicates that agency's discovery in some detail. On Wednesday, October 13, 1976, Robinson—a retired school superintendent and prominent Palestine civil rights leader— was killed by a single 12-gauge shotgun blast to his forehead. The barrel of the gun had reportedly been pressed directly against the flesh covering the bridge of his nose between his eyeballs. The top and right sides of his head were blown away. The physical evidence, mostly confined to the front half of the left bay of the two-car garage adjacent to and behind the Robinson residence, was described as follows:

> *Body was laying on its back in a sprawled position, feet slightly spread, left hand laying on the left side of chest, and right arm laying back, pointed upward. Victim was fully clothed, top part of head blown away from obvious shotgun wound. Brain matter and blood were on the walls surrounding the body, and on the floor surrounding same. Head was resting against closed screen door* [approximately halfway down the left wall of the garage bay] *which entered into the house from garage.*
>
> *A 12 gauge, double barrel, sawed off shotgun, SN X4313, Ranger brand, was found with stock resting on victim's legs, and barrel laying onto the concrete floor. In the chamber of the shotgun was found one spent round and one live round, both of #8 shot, Remington Peters ammunition, with spent round being in left barrel.*
>
> *There were two spent shells found on the ground, both of the same caliber and brand and shot number as was found in the weapon. One was found beside the right arm of the victim and the other one was found approximately three feet from the victim.*

The new, red 1976 Oldsmobile belonging to Frank's wife, Dorothy, was parked in the right bay of the garage, and in front of it sat a gasoline rototiller and a lawn vacuum sweeper. The bag for the sweeper was draped over the handle of the rototiller. Ranger Prince's report indicated that the rototiller, the lawn vacuum sweeper bag and the front fender of Dorothy's car all had shot damage. Some of the shot had struck the catalytic converter and muffler under the vehicle, and some had ricocheted off the front bumper and lodged in the back wall of the garage.

FRANK AND DOROTHY ROBINSON's residence sat on a hill just west of the A.M. Story Middle School (formerly the A.M. Story High School) and north of most of the rest of the neighborhood, which was called Haven Acres. Robinson dabbled in real estate and had developed Haven Acres himself. One of the streets that led into the neighborhood was named Robinson, and another bore Dorothy's maiden name, Redus. The playground for the A.M. Story Middle School sat below the front of the Robinson residence, between the school itself and Variah ("Vibrant Life"), the street the Robinsons lived at the end of. On the day Frank Robinson was killed, six boys were playing football on that playground and actually heard or saw something relevant to the man's death.

The six boys who provided details were James David Allen, eleven, white; David Warden Brown, twelve, white; Charles Hardy Gregory III, eleven, white; Jeffrey Todd Kale, eleven, white; Carlos Aaron Sepulveda, twelve, Hispanic; and Donald Eugene Watkins, thirteen, white. All six heard four shots, and Hawkins said he saw a white man standing behind Robinson's fence when the last couple of shots were fired. Earlier that morning, A.M. Story student Michael Kevin Peterson, eleven, white, said he saw a white man in a white van leaving the Robinson residence.

After local law enforcement officers completed their crime scene analysis, Palestine Police chief Kenneth Berry—who had been on the job eighteen months after seventeen years with the Waco Police Department—announced that the official autopsy revealed no traces of gunpowder residue on Robinson's body and termed his death a homicide.[2] He reiterated this conclusion on Thursday, October 14,[3] and by Friday, October 15, the police had issued a public plea for help in the investigation of the "shotgun slaying." Chief Berry said, "We have no suspects, but we do have leads we are working on."

Dorothy and Frank Robinson
at Prairie View A&M
University in 1930, four weeks
before they were married.
Photo by Dorothy Redus Robinson.

By that following Monday (October 18), however, Chief Berry's mind had changed. Within a week of Robinson's death, Berry was claiming that an absence of nitrate or gunpowder residue on a person who fired a shotgun was not uncommon and that the police had "run out of leads,"[4] could establish no motives and had no witnesses (a statement that the six white, young witnesses from A.M. Story arguably made a clear prevarication). And in a matter of days, many whites in the community already accepted the narrative that Robinson's wounds were self-inflicted, while most Blacks contended that the incident was an assassination. Dr. John Warfield, a University of Texas professor, told the *Austin American-Statesman* that "Black people there have little faith in the police department" because Palestine police offers weren't in the habit of upholding justice where Blacks were concerned.[5]

State representative Paul Ragsdale (D-Dallas) also spoke with the *Statesman*, and his sentiments echoed Warfield's. "The people there are very much concerned that it is a possible political assassination."[6]

Warfield, after whom the John L. Warfield Center for African and African American Studies at the University of Texas–Austin is now named, expounded on his remarks to the *Statesman*. "It is clear that this Ku Klux Klan–style murder and terror is as real on the 200th birthday of this immature nation as it was in the 19th century. There is a conspiracy in this state to obstruct the political rights and the political awakening of Black and brown people and the powerful potential constituency they represent."[7]

And Warfield's political conspiracy reference was directly aimed at sitting Texas governor Dolph Briscoe, who had vocally opposed President Lyndon Baines Johnson's 1965 Voting Rights Act and referred to South Texas as a "little Cuba" just a month earlier.

Warfield also told the *Statesman* that he thought the assassin had waited for Robinson in the office connecting the house with the garage and observed that "these are the kinds of things that create a climate that legitimizes the thing that happened to Frank."

Ragsdale noted that many locals believed Robinson's death was the result of a sanctioned hit executed by a hired killer from somewhere else.

It was mid-July 2022 when I got a phone call from Davies, an award-winning San Antonio journalist. Since 1999, he had been the host and producer of *Texas Matters*, a weekly radio news magazine and podcast in which he examines the questions and issues facing the Lone Star State. Davies had done pieces on the Slocum Massacre after my book on the subject came out in 2014 and while I was working with the descendants of that pogrom for a historical marker. The marker effort was a grueling, uphill battle, but it proved successful in the end, thanks in no small part to journalists like Davies, who covered it for NPR. I think we both knew then that there was still work to be done.

I had pushed along with Constance Hollie-Jawaid, a descendant of victims of the bloodshed, to raise awareness about the atrocity and remind people that the victims of the massacre were still buried in unmarked mass graves. And something that was said when we first met with Anderson County Historical Commission Chairman Jimmie Ray Odom about the approved marker stunned us.

Frank J. Robinson had known Abe Wilson, a Hollie-Jawaid forebear directly affected by the Slocum Massacre, and Robinson had, again, gone on to become a local civil rights champion. In fact, he and two other Black men from Palestine, Rodney A. Howard and Timothy Smith, had sued the Anderson County Commissioners Court over race-based gerrymandering and won their suit in Smith County Federal Court in 1973[8] and prevailed again on December 23, 1974, when Anderson County challenged the ruling in the Fifth Circuit Court of Appeals.[9] Robinson, Howard and Smith's attorney had been Dave Richards, the husband of former Texas governor Ann Richards. And Port Arthur native Irving Loeb Goldberg, the circuit judge who authored the decision, did not hide his disdain for the wiles of Anderson County:

> *This case results from a gerrymander of precinct lines in Anderson County, Texas, to dilute the black vote in County Commissioner elections. Unfortunately, the disrespect of voting rights is not a recent innovation in county government in Texas.....Nor, unfortunately, is unconstitutional dilution of voting rights only a very old part of our history....Caesar found Gaul divided into three parts. Here, we are confronted with a County Commissioners Court which has cut the county's black community into three illogical parts in order to dilute the black vote in precinct elections, acting as a modern Caesar dissecting its private Gaul. Such apportionment poisons our representative democracy at its roots. Our constitution cannot abide it.*

Robinson, Smith and Howard didn't stop there. They immediately began working on a lawsuit to establish single-member districts in Palestine so the local Black vote would also be protected in city council elections. Austin

Anderson County Council of Black Farmers in 1933. Frank Robinson is front and center in leather boots. *Photo by Dorothy Redus Robinson.*

attorney Larry Daves worked with the trio on this suit, and in late 1975, they achieved a consent decree that forced Palestine into redistricting. The trio's efforts opened up Anderson County to Black political representation and a say in how the community was run and how the county was governed.

Then, in mid- to late 1976, Robinson began working on (among other things) a local scandal, specifically reports that Black citizens who lived north of him were being charged for city services that they didn't receive. It became the next injustice that he turned his attention to. On Labor Day weekend of that year, he expressed as much to longtime friends Sidney Earl and Vita Childs Palmer, whom Robinson and Dorothy had known since their college days at Prairie View A&M University. The Palmers' daughter, Eloyce Green, had grown up referring to the Robinsons as "Uncle Frank" and "Aunt Dorothy," and she remembered Robinson discussing the scandal with her father at their home in Tyler during a Labor Day visit.

"I can still see my parents talking to Frank in the kitchen," Green, eighty-two, told me. "My dad told him, 'If you don't leave these white folks alone, they're gonna kill you.'"

Frank's response was simple and straightforward. "I'm not afraid 'cause they won't be getting nothing but an old man."

DAVIES AND I HAD both been watching the current Texas legislature's ongoing gerrymandering tactics with various and, I'm sure, comparable levels of consternation and dismay. And we were both aware of Frank J. Robinson's work and genuinely troubled by the ways in which the current Republican attempts to ensure white electoral primacy undermined everything Robinson had fought and probably died for. Robinson believed Blacks ought to have a say. He believed Blacks should have a seat at the table. The most recent Republican-apportioned voting maps seemed flagrantly designed to limit the voices of persons of color in particular.

So, Davies called me in mid-July to discuss researching the suspicious circumstances surrounding Robinson's death. He said he was working on an October piece for the *Texas Observer* and an NPR podcast examining the subject in more detail. He noted that when he discussed the details of his story with the *Observer*, they suggested he reach out to me.

Staff members at the Austin-based bimonthly were aware of my book *The 1910 Slocum Massacre: An Act of Genocide in East Texas* and my work with massacre descendants to get the historical marker. Former *Observer* staffer Michael Barajas had also written a powerful feature on the unmarked mass graves in the Slocum area, "Where the Bodies Are Buried," in the July–August 2019 edition of the magazine. And three months later, I was mentioned in the October *Texas Monthly* cover story, "The Battle to Rewrite Texas History," as part of a new generation of writers and scholars trying to set the record straight.[10] Then, when American conservatives declared critical race theory (CRT) public enemy number one, I wrote about meeting Anderson County Historical Commission chairman Odom with Slocum Massacre descendant Hollie-Jawaid in the July 7, 2021 edition of the *Fort Worth Weekly*:

> *In late December 2015, Constance Hollie-Jawaid and I were still working on the final plans for the dedication ceremony for a Texas state historical marker commemorating the Slocum Massacre. The fight to get the marker approved had been grueling, and, on that particular day, we had traveled to Palestine, Texas, to meet with the marker effort's chief antagonist, Anderson County Historical Chairman Jimmy Ray Odom. Odom's beliefs about the Slocum Massacre were almost completely contradictory to ours, but—in conversation, anyway—he was a straight shooter. Our historical and cultural disagreements notwithstanding, I respected him for that.*
>
> *Jimmy had taken some heat in the press for his straight-shooting, and he was upset with me. And when we met that day in late December, he let me know this in no uncertain terms. At that point, however, the marker was secured. Constance—a descendant of victims of the atrocity—and I had won the argument, so we could be magnanimous. I let Jimmy air his grievances without response or complaint....After the discussion regarding the marker ceremony concluded and the air was a hair more convivial, I asked Jimmy why there was no historical marker for a Black activist named Frank J. Robinson—and his response was as straightforward as it was shocking.*
>
> *"Oh, they killed him," Jimmy said.*

The statement was dumbfounding.

Odom and the historical commission had so adamantly opposed our Slocum Massacre marker that we were forced to sidestep Anderson County and appeal directly to the Texas State Historical Commission. And because Odom and the local commission had engaged in so many ridiculous machinations and stall tactics, the state consented to our request. And here Odom was, unwilling to concede an atrocity committed

115 years earlier but flatly acknowledging an assassination just 40 years previous.

I had planned to do more research into Frank J. Robinson's death at that time and maybe even write a book on the subject, but one project or another interfered or led me on to other stories.

By the middle of last year, Davies had begun his own research on Robinson's "questionable death." A few months before my piece in the *Fort Worth Weekly*, he had requested records pertaining to Robinson's death from the Palestine Police Department. On May 26, 2021, Donna Thornell, one of the department's administrative assistants, responded with a short letter informing Davies that "due to the age of this case, there are no files available/located with the Palestine Police Department pertaining to Mr. Robinson."

Davies, then—like me—got busy with other projects, and it was a year before he picked it back up and contacted me for an assist and an extra eye on the case.

HATE CRIME.

It's a fairly new legal term in this country, but it was made a criminal offense by Texan president Lyndon Baines Johnson in Title I of the 1968 Civil Rights Act. It became against the law to use, or threaten to use, force to willfully interfere with any person because of race, color, religion or national origin, especially when that person is participating in a federally protected activity, such as attending school, patronizing a public place/facility, applying for employment or acting as a juror in a state court or voting. This was 103 years after the end of the Civil War.

As I left my west Fort Worth home, veered east and headed for Palestine, my mind was jumbled with thoughts on this subject. When I began my journey on I-20, I recalled that a group of Fort Worth citizens had actually traveled to Kansas in 1860 to seize Anthony Bewley, a white abolitionist pastor, and return him to Cowtown to publicly lynch him. Rumors still persist that following Bewley's September 13, 1860 lynching, his bones were prominently displayed at a local business for years after the act.

As I exited I-20 and headed southeast on 287 South, I remembered that the City of Mansfield had refused to desegregate its schools for a decade after desegregation became federal law.

A year after my book on the Slocum Massacre was released, I published *Black Holocaust: The Paris Horror and a Legacy of Texas Terror* with Eakin Press. In it, I detailed the circumstances and facts about the dozens of persons of color

Assassinated Black civil rights leaders, including Medgar Evers, Malcolm X, Martin Luther King Jr. and Frank J. Robinson (*bottom right*). *Composition by author.*

who were literally burned at the stake in Texas. And, as 287 led me through Midlothian, I thought of Steve Davis, an innocent Black man burned at the stake in the Waxahachie area on May 12, 1912. Then, when I finally reached I-45 and turned south, I was soon greeted by a new billboard inviting tourists to stop in Corsicana. It labeled the town "Texas's Favorite Detour," which disturbed me, because I knew it hadn't been for an innocent Black man named Jonas "John" Henderson. He was pulled off a train headed for Fort Worth in Hillsboro, transported to Corsicana and ceremonially burned at the stake in the town square on March 13, 1901, for allegedly murdering a white woman he may never have met. There's a photo collection in the Dallas Public Library that documents the incident![11]

Corsicana's new billboard struck me the wrong way. It was morbid. Or maybe I was being morbid.

At Corsicana, I exited and turned left to finish the drive to Palestine on 287 South, and then it started all over again. A few miles past the Richland-Chambers Reservoir, I saw a sign for Kerens, where a Black man had been mysteriously burned alive in the town jail on December 13, 1890. And a little farther down, I saw a sign announcing a right turn for the Freestone County seat, Fairfield, where three innocent Black men— Johnnie Cornish, Snap Curry and Mose Jones—were seized from the county jail, transported fourteen miles west to Kirven and burned at the stake one after another in the wee hours of May 7, 1922, for the alleged murder of a young white woman.

Was it any wonder that so many of us consciously or subconsciously averted our eyes to this history? Didn't it sabotage everything we'd been taught to believe about ourselves, our state and even our country?

I ARRIVED IN PALESTINE midmorning on Friday, July 29, 2022, and the early steps in the investigation that Davies and I took were inauspicious. Davies's preliminary research indicated that the Robinson residence was directly behind the relatively new A.M. Story Intermediate School but said the street they lived on was no longer there. My initial research focused on the street itself and indicated it was still there. So, off we went in search of the former Robinson residence, 819 Variah. It was still there; we confirmed it with images from old newspaper clippings. But the A.M. Story Middle School was gone, having become a large, overgrown vacant lot. I thought it was strange. Generally speaking, school districts repurpose buildings instead of razing them, especially if they have historical significance.

Alonzo Marion Story came to Texas from Louisiana at the age of twenty-one and taught math in a little town called Midway before moving to Palestine in 1912. He taught math at the community's Black high school, Lincoln High School, for five years and then took a job as the superintendent of the state's Deaf, Dumb, and Blind Institute for Colored

Youth. In 1924, he returned to Lincoln and served as the principal and a math teacher until his retirement in 1949. In 1953, the Palestine Independent School District opened the Alonzo Marion Story High School for Blacks. After desegregation, the facility became a junior high—which it was at the time of Robinson's death—and then an elementary school. But as Davies quickly uncovered, the original A.M. Story building was demolished by a tornado on November 15, 1987. It was rebuilt as an intermediate school at a different location in 1990. The Category 3 cataclysm traveled two hundred miles on that November day, leaving several dead and millions of dollars of destruction in its wake, but it had passed right in front of Frank and Dorothy's old house without leaving so much as a scratch.

The most recent owners of the Robinsons' former residence were out when we came by, so we examined the house and the adjacent two-car garage from the street and then drove around Haven Acres. The name of the main access street running in front of Haven Acres had been changed. It was now known as Martin Luther King Jr. Boulevard, and Robinson Avenue intersected it at the 1700 block. This was encouraging and grist for a discussion of bizarre serendipity versus simple happenstance. A questionable, controversial death. A tornadic rampage that destroyed the historic school. And then the community's MLK Boulevard placed and dedicated right down the hill from the scene of the possible crime and a subsequent natural disaster. It figuratively—if not literally—reeked of a guilty community. Neither Davies nor I are superstitious, but it seemed almost silly to assume it was a coincidence.

We made our way to the Anderson County Courthouse and spent most of the rest of the day shuttling back and forth between the bowels of the courthouse and Palestine City Hall. The staff members were great, but we got nowhere. There were no folders, no files and no relevant paperwork. We spent hours in the courthouse basement, thumbing through multiple tomes of legal documents but found nothing pertinent. Frustrated, we pressed the assistants in the Anderson County Clerk's office, and they referred us to the county clerk himself, Mark Staples. We'd contacted Staples beforehand, and he, in fact, was the one who sent us to the basement file room. Coincidence or not, he was out the day we told him we'd be there. A couple of city hall staff members subsequently referred us to the office of James Todd, justice of the peace, Precinct 3. Todd, sixty-eight, had been a JP in Anderson County since 1985 and, before that, the chief of police in Elkhart. They thought he might know something or be able to help us.

Dorothy and Frank Robinson presented with a plaque for political leadership from Prairie View A&M by state representative Paul Ragsdale on August 4, 1976. *Photo by Dorothy Redus Robinson.*

Todd's courthouse office was lined with baseball bats and sports memorabilia. He was personable, knowledgeable and forthcoming. Well aware of the controversial investigation into Robinson's death, Todd was unequivocal. "It stinks to high heaven," he said of the suicide ruling.

Davies and I questioned him about the reported four shots, noting the 12-gauge shotgun's two-shell capacity, and asked whether it was feasible that Robinson could have fired the double-barrel, break-action shotgun four times, cracking it open to remove spent shells and reload without getting gunpowder residue on his person. Todd succinctly confirmed what other law enforcement officers I had spoken with had already told me. It was practically impossible.

Listening in, Todd's secretary said we should talk to County Judge Jeff Doran. Doran, seventy-one, was also personable and amicable, and he agreed with Todd. Though he wasn't in the area at the time, he commented that the results of the virtually unprecedented inquest into the cause of

Robinson's death weren't universally well received in the community, and he conceded that many Anderson County citizens, Black and white, felt and still feel that the local justice system got it wrong. Then, as the discussion proceeded, Davies and I asked him about the imposing Reagan Park statue of John Reagan, the former postmaster of the Confederacy and the first railroad commissioner of Texas. Following his release from prison after the Civil War, Reagan returned to Palestine and quickly became unpopular. He told his fellow former Confederates to go along with the occupying Union troops. His former compatriots mistakenly viewed him as a traitor, but Reagan was playing the long game. He knew that the sooner the citizens of Palestine complied, the sooner the Union troops would leave and Palestine could get back to going about its business—especially where the Black population was concerned. Reagan was omnipresent in the community, but there was nary a hint of progressive folks like Frank J. Robinson, who was certainly one of the state's most important civil rights leaders. Palestine hardly claimed him.

On that point, Doran was starkly realistic. "You have to understand. Before the Civil War, Palestine was the fourth-largest city in the state."

He noted that it had even donated some of its early horse-drawn trolleys to its "little sister" city, Dallas, and that the most valuable asset Palestine and Anderson County possessed in those days was its slave population— its enslaved persons were worth more than anything else in the economy. And after the Civil War, the most valuable asset the community had was eradicated. Doran didn't shill for the Confederacy, but he did say that Reagan brought the railroad to Palestine after its economy had been flattened and ensured the city's prosperity for the next 150 years.

DAVIES AND I THEN tracked down Ben Campbell, eighty-one, a local historian and the recent author of *Two Railroads Two Towns*. Campbell confirmed Doran's comments about John Reagan and the railroad, but he also echoed Todd's and Doran's general sentiments about Frank J. Robinson's death.

"It doesn't pass the smell test," he said. "It wasn't a suicide."

When Davies and I solicited his opinion on why Robinson's accomplishments, legacy and horrific end were so little known, he was frank. "The Black community knows about it," he said, noting that hardly anyone outside of that demographic (or even Frank's generation) reflects on the incident. "It was over and done. People don't talk about it."

IT WAS A CONTEMPLATIVE evening for me. Outside of a handwritten, unilluminating paragraph or two in a ledger provided to us by Todd, we found no other investigation documents or evidence. More questions than answers.

As previously noted, Palestine Police chief Berry declared Robinson's death a murder and then reclassified it as a suicide because he somehow straight-facedly reasoned that the police department could establish no motive for a homicide. And on October 20, he told the *Austin American-Statesman* that "no one saw anybody near [Robinson's] house the day he died," even though testimonies to the contrary submitted by five white middle schoolers and one Hispanic child were already part of the investigative record. Berry's perspective on the case did not jibe with that of Roy Herrington, the longtime Anderson County sheriff. The disagreement between Berry and Herrington (now both deceased), other inconsistencies and outside parties comparing Robinson's convenient demise to the assassinations of Medgar Evers and Martin Luther King Jr. led to a special inquest of the incident.

None of the sitting justices of the peace had law degrees, and somehow the case fell to thirty-year-old municipal court judge Alexander Nemer II. On October 20, 1976, it was announced that a formal inquest before a six-person "coroner's jury" would be held in the next five to ten days.[12] Nemer

The house of Frank and Dorothy Redus Robinson is still standing in Palestine. *Photo by author.*

instructed Chief Berry and others that a "gag rule" would be imposed on every trial participant to prevent them from elaborating on their testimony after the inquest was over.[13]

The next day, Nemer pushed the inquest date out to November 16. On October 28, two Texas legislators called for the inquest to be expanded to a full homicide investigation. State Representative Mickey Leland (D-Houston) said the current treatment of the case was inadequate. "I feel there is something shady going on," Leland said. "I think it smells of an inkling of a cover-up in the way Mr. Robinson was killed." Ragsdale's comments were more pointed. "The black citizens of this state will not stand for a cover-up in the search for Frank's killer," he said. "The moment it appears that this investigation is falling short of the mark, I intend to call for the FBI to intervene and take it over."[14]

Leland claimed that Robinson was one of the most effective civil rights advocates in the state and that his efforts to empower Blacks ran contrary to those of the current powers that be. "It was a political murder," Leland said.[15]

ON NOVEMBER 15, 1976—ELEVEN years to the day the 1987 tornado tore through Palestine—the unsequestered inquest jurists were empaneled. The postponed inquest commenced the next morning.

In the newspapers of the day, it went well for Palestine. The whole city seemed to be on trial, and, in the end, Robinson's suicide acquitted the white community and absolved the long-standing cultural institutions that whites cherished. Nemer's inquest was conducted by local attorneys Richard Handorf and Melvin Whitaker, with assistance from State Assistant Attorney General Anthony Sadberry, an African American. In a 1982 interview with the *Fort Worth Star-Telegram*, Sadberry indicated that "he was bound by his profession to accept the ruling of the court" unless he could produce "concrete, conflicting evidence," and he couldn't. But he wasn't satisfied. Of his cohorts and the leaders of the community in general, Sadberry remarked that they seemed "very interested in vindicating that town." In fact, he noted this in comments during an Associated Press interview that ran in the November 3, 1976 edition of the *Dallas Morning News*. "From the physical evidence we have," Sadberry said, "you couldn't make or break either theory [homicide or suicide]. Seemingly, there is an effort by authorities who stress suicide as though the evidence should support that. I think the approach should be objective.

Statue of John H. Reagan, postmaster of the Confederacy and the first railroad commissioner of Texas. Reagan is omnipresent in Palestine. *Photo by author.*

With regard to suicide, you can't make that statement as a matter of law."

When the inquest commenced, evidence contradicting the homicide theory was blatantly ignored, and every narrative that bolstered the suicide theory was stressed. The testimony of A.M. Story middle schoolers was discounted, and a local mortician who claimed that Robinson's body was "tampered with" at the scene of the crime was never called to testify. The testimony of Robinson's wife, Dorothy—a chairwoman of the Texas Advisory Council for Technical Vocational Education and a recent recipient of an achievement award from the National Association of Negro Business and Professional Women Clubs, who was in Minnesota at the time of her husband's death—was hardly an obstruction for what her attorney, Dave Richards, later described as a "steamroller" toward a foregone conclusion. In his 2002 book *Once Upon a Time in Texas: A Liberal in the Lone Star State*, Richards writes, "There was no evidence to support the suicide theory, no notes, no indication of despondency or health problems. Yet the power structure apparently could not live with the murder alternative and were committed to the suicide rationale. The trial was so painful and the atmosphere so tense that much of it is blotted from my mind."

The principal players couldn't even get their stories straight. Chief Berry testified at the inquest that there was no evidence of an intruder at the Robinson home. The October Texas Ranger report that indicated a three-inch hole approximately eighteen inches up in the screen door leading from the garage into the house was discovered the day of the incident. Tests were run on Frank Robinson's shoes to see if he had kicked the screen during a struggle or while falling down. The hole was not made by his shoes, and though the screen was reportedly new, there was no explanation for the damage. Except that a three-inch slit eighteen inches up on the screen door would have allowed someone to reach up through the screen and disengage or reengage the screen door latch.

Chief Berry also said that after Robinson shot himself, the shotgun was found lying across Robinson's left leg, with the barrel pointing to the left. Justice of the Peace Floyd Hassell, however, testified that the shotgun barrel was pointing right. Arguably, the point is moot. Firing a shotgun is like firing a small cannon. That's why you prop the shotgun stock firmly against your shoulder. If you fail to do so, the shotgun—like a small cannon—will kick backward. In the case of a shotgun, this will result in injuring or bruising your shoulder or, if you're not heavy or strong enough, knocking you down. So if you fire a 12-gauge shotgun at your own face with the barrel resting on your forehead and one hand presumably holding it while the other is used to pull a trigger (presumably with a thumb), it will kick backward after firing and fly out of your hands and away from your body altogether.

Sadberry, now deceased, was haunted by the inquest's outcome. "I can't say in my own mind I am satisfied with the outcome of the inquest," he told the *Star-Telegram* in 1982. "I don't feel sure about what took place."

FIRST UP FOR DAVIES and me on Saturday, July 30, was a local Black historian named Norris White. Soft-spoken, cautious and thoughtful, White wanted to make sure we knew he hadn't come to Palestine until the early 1990s, and when he found out about what Frank J. Robinson and others had achieved, he was shocked by the absence of any real recognition of those achievements or indignance about Robinson's death. A fifty-four-year-old academic with some edge, White prefaced his interview with us by laying out several books that he felt explained the history of the Black experience in East Texas. One of them was my book on the Slocum Massacre. I was flattered but more impressed by some of his recent efforts, which paralleled ours. In February 2018, he published a story about Robinson's accomplishments in the *Palestine Herald-Press*, and it cost him a job. Undeterred, he dug further into Robinson's death and spoke with six local Blacks and one white, ranging in age from their sixties to eighties. And what they agreed to share was communicated only under Norris's promise of complete confidentiality. After those conversations, including two with Black men who had been middle schoolers at A.M. Story when Robinson was killed (and who corroborated the white middle schoolers' accounts) but knew better than to come forward, Norris was emphatic.

"The history of East Texas speaks for itself," he said. "There are no intricate plots. The plot is, 'Let's go kill that nigger.' It may be 160 years since the Civil War ended, and post–civil rights, but the mindset is the same."

The sense that White got from everyone he interviewed was remarkably similar. "Mr. Robinson was a guy for everybody, and to a lot of people, that's what's so hurtful about it."

White and the folks he interviewed suggest that that's what is most shameful. For the past forty-seven years, nobody has really done anything about what many perceive to be Frank's assassination, and they feel like the community has let Robinson down. But Norris White isn't naive. "Lemme tell you, when I first got here, this was the running joke: 'Black may be beautiful, and tan may be grand, but white is the color of the big boss man.' In other words, 'Don't step out of line, nigger.' And that's the sentiment. That's East Texas. That's the East Texas I worked under 30 years ago, and that's the East Texas I live in today."

Norris White's comments and the strict confidence he had to offer in order to obtain his information brought to mind another confidential

The Confederate Stars and Bars flag is still popular in Palestine, Texas. *Photo by author.*

informant with whom Davies and I had both spoken on separate occasions. The source would say a lot but nothing on record. They had been involved in the local justice system and Anderson County historical circles. They had actually questioned a member of the local judiciary who had been an attorney involved in the Robinson inquest about the unconvincing outcome, and that individual, who was then a sitting judge, cautioned the source in no uncertain terms to leave it alone. He even threatened to charge the source with contempt of court.

Davies and I finished the day trying to locate other interviewees but without much luck. We wanted to speak with Rodney A. Howard, the surviving member of the trio who had challenged and defeated the gerrymandering regime of Anderson County and Palestine on two separate occasions, but he was busy and hard to pin down. I thought, like Norris White's anonymous sources, and ours, that Howard was reticent to speak publicly. And I understood why.

We located a seventy-three-year-old Black man whom Frank J. Robinson had mentored and who would speak on the record instead. His name was James Robert Smith. The Palestine NAACP secretary at the time of Robinson's death, Smith rejected the inquest's determination. "I believe it was a setup related to an undercurrent of old money. Frank was causing a rift that these people didn't want."

Smith believed Frank was killed and his death was made to look like a suicide to discredit him. "Suicide is like voodoo taboo [for Black people], so we don't do that."

Later, collating, considering and weighing the interviews and information we'd collected so far led to another heady night. Over the last decade, I'd spent a lot of time researching and writing about some incredibly dark history in East Texas, and Robinson and his cohorts appeared to have been proverbial beacons of light. And now, forty-seven years after his sketchy death, I'd met nothing but Palestine citizens—Black and white—who didn't believe Robinson had committed suicide.

It was unfamiliar, heartening territory.

DAVIES AND I SPOKE with Nemer the following Sunday morning. As late as 2017, he had served again as a municipal court judge in Palestine, and he had actually just campaigned unsuccessfully to become the town's next mayor.

Friendly and well-spoken, Nemer was possessed of an uncanny recollection of the inquest proceedings. "I knew one day that exactly what we're doing would come to pass," he said.

PAUL B. RAGSDALE
DISTRICT 33N
AUSTIN OFFICE
STATE CAPITOL
BOX 2910
AUSTIN, TEXAS 78767
512/475-5923

House of Representatives
Austin, Texas
May 19, 1976

DISTRICT OFFICE
5710 EAST R.L. THORNTON FWY
DALLAS, TEXAS
214/827-1750

Mr. Frank Robinson
Box 1212
Palestine, Tx   75801

Dear Frank:

The East Texas Project needs your help!

My office is in the process of coordinating the filing
of some thirteen lawsuits similar to the Anderson County
syit all across East Texas. The counties under suit include:
Camp, Fallas, Freestone, Gregg, Limestone, Marion, Matogorda,
Morris, Robertson, San Augustine, San Jacinto and Washington
counties.

As you know, the East Texas Leadership Forum has
active memberships in several of these counties. In fact,
several of our plaintiffs are active members-Vice President
Leveren Everett, B.T. Hogan, and E. E. Wheat. I am requesting
that you contact these men, and any other members in these
and other counties, soliciting financial support for the Project.
We were in hopes that each county undersuit could at least
contribute $100. We need this money to defray legal expenses,
pay student interns who work with the project and to provide
funding for staff travel and expert witnesses during trials.

Let me add here that these suits in no way represent the
end of the East Texas Project. We still have several more
counties to file against. Additionally we plan to shift
our emphasis from these county suits to focus on obtaining
Single Member Districts for the city councils, and school
districts of the major towns and cities across East Texas.
This, too, will need substantial financial support.

I appreciate you past efforts to put the East Texas
Project on a sound financial basis. But I still need your
help. I hope you will do what you can to provide the badly
needed funds for this important effort.

Sincerely,

Paul

Paul B. Ragsdale

P. S. Checks made payable to Paul B. Ragsdale Special Projects Fund.

Evidentiary letter that confirms Representative Ragsdale, Robinson, et al. were definitely
expanding their fight against racial gerrymandering across East Texas. *Public domain.*

He knew someone would eventually show up at his door asking questions about Robinson's death. And he admitted that county officials needed someone to handle the inquest and that the thirty-year-old "was the easiest mark available."

But he insisted that the inquest went where the evidence led it and stood by the inquest's declaration of suicide. Nemer also claimed he "knew Frank as well as anybody" and that the political establishment in Anderson County was "not the least bit afraid of Mr. Frank. Period."

Davies wasn't having it. We both knew Robinson had been working with Ragsdale on something bigger. "Robinson and Ragsdale were getting ready to expand on their successes," Davies said, "where they would take what Frank had done here and move it to eleven different counties across East Texas… and so, though he presented himself as a nonthreatening figure, he was actually doing incredible things through the courts and bringing about the empowerment of African American communities throughout East Texas."

"I certainly would agree with that," Nemer replied. "That's the truth."

"And you don't think some people didn't like that?" Davies said.

"I can't speak for them," Nemer responded, like an implacable totem of the old guard.

"Well," Davies continued, "how do you think Frank should be remembered?"

"First, I think Frank J. Robinson should be remembered as a good person," Nemer said. "Second, I think he should be remembered as a community activist who led the way to doing a lot of good and, ultimately, brought the Black and white communities together. It takes leaders to accomplish things, and he certainly, absolutely, positively was a leader who did his darn level best to accomplish that. He felt like it was his mission, and he did it to the best of his ability."

WHEN DAVIES AND I finally sat down with Rodney Howard and told him Nemer had a high opinion of Robinson but still stood by the inquest verdict, Howard spoke very plainly. "He would. Quite a few of them, that's the spin they wanted to put on it."

Howard, eighty, had worked with his elders Robinson and Timothy Smith in the early to mid-1970s as an energetic protégé, young but equal and willing to put in the work and stick with it. A civil rights champion in his own right, he didn't waste time with platitudes. When we told him that Nemer dismissed the notion that the local powers that be ever sweated

Left to right, Anderson County civil rights heroes Timothy S. Smith, Rodney A. Howard and Frank J. Robinson (circa 1976). *Public domain..*

Robinson and, by extension, the work of the trio, he almost grinned. "Well, I think Frank was a big threat because they didn't wanna see the county change. We were working on a level of political power that they didn't want us to have."

In a recent phone call with Daves, the trio's attorney in their final case against the Palestine City Council, the retired lawyer agreed. "Robinson was a threat in the sense that he was taking on the status quo, and he was trying to drag the community into the modern age. There was a long, long history of white supremacy there, and the atmosphere was intimidating. I think Frank was a threat to the power structure there because he was trying to undo the last one hundred years of history in the region."

Howard mourns his old friend Frank and doesn't believe the "official" version of Robinson's demise. "What reason did Frank have to kill himself? He totally caught his wife off guard. He caught the Black community off guard. He caught all the people who worked with him off guard. He and Dorothy were not struggling. They were living decent. I didn't see anything that would indicate that he would go off his rocker and do something like that. He had too much to live for and be proud of."

Howard and Timothy Smith had also received death threats back then, and Howard went a stretch or two sleeping on the floor on the side of his bed farthest from a window with any weapons he had at his side.

"I think he was killed, myself," Howard said. "Those of us who were close to him and worked with him...we knew he was too much of a fighter to do something like that."

LATER, AFTER A STORY I wrote on Frank's murder was published in *Fort Worth Weekly* and Davies had already finished three episodes of his podcast on the subject, *The Ghost of Frank J. Robinson*, I revisited the Briscoe Center for American History at the University of Texas–Austin. I was in the Capital City for the Texas Book Festival, which began the next day.

I went through the Frank J. Robinson and Dorothy Redus Robinson Papers collection again, and something startling jumped out at me. Alex Nemer had been an attorney for Anderson County in the 1973 lawsuit Robinson, Smith and Howard filed against Anderson County?!

This was information he failed to disclose in our interview. This was information that rendered his remarks to the effect that Anderson County leaders were "not the least bit afraid of Mr. Frank" hollow.

If they weren't afraid, why did they appeal the original decision? And if Alex Nemer had served as an Anderson County attorney arguing against Robinson, Smith and Howard's case, shouldn't he have recused himself from the inquest hearing?

That option wouldn't have been popular.

The hearing would then probably have been conducted by someone outside the county and maybe even by someone without "skin" in the outcome.

AND YET.

Frank J. Robinson is gone, and his legend doesn't really live on. The past several incarnations of the Texas legislature verge on violating Title I of the 1968 Civil Rights Act every other session, making a mockery of everything Robinson stood for, fought for and died for—and most Texans, Black or white, don't even know his name.

2

FOR WHOM THE OIL TOLLS

Nearly 1,000 journalists from other countries reported from Spain at some point during the war, filing hundreds of thousands of words in a dozen or more languages describing the majestic, beautiful city under siege, suffering the ravages of prolonged aerial bombing. Yet, strangely, these reporters missed a huge story. Not one of them, it appears, looked up at the droning, V-shaped formations of Hitler's Junkers in the sky above Madrid and wondered: whose fuel is powering those aircraft?
—Adam Hochschild, *Spain in Our Hearts: Americans in the Spanish Civil War, 1936–1939*

T orkild Rieber.
It's a name you'd think folks might remember. Perhaps as the alias of a dastardly comic book villain or the name of a bad seed from a pulp fiction crime thriller. But he was much worse and more real than characters like that. He was the head of the Texas Company (or Texas Corp.) in the mid- to late 1930s. But he did make the cover of *Time* magazine on May 4, 1936.

Rieber was a Norwegian émigré who had taken to the sea at the age of fourteen, earned a maritime master license at nineteen and got his first command as the captain of a Texas Company oil freighter at the age of twenty-one. He transported oil for the company (frequently out of Port Arthur) for four years, and he came "ashore to superintend the conversion" of a New Jersey peach orchard into a "great" Texas Company oil terminal.

Children emerge from a sewer in Madrid after German bombing in support of Spanish fascists in 1937. *Public domain*.

From there, he steadily moved up the Texas Corp. ranks, and *Time* described him as a man of "horse sense, a command of men," a man with "a maze of wrinkles around his grey eyes earned by years of gazing at ten times ten thousand miles of changing seas" and "forthright, generous, usually genial, sometimes convivial." At the time, Rieber was putting the finishing touches on a deal to make billions of dollars off crude-oil investments in Venezuela. He followed this up with betting on a coup in Spain.

JUST A FEW MONTHS shy of the one hundredth anniversary of Texas's independence from Mexico, a confederation of conservative fascists attempted to overthrow the liberal Republican government of Spain. A bloody Guerra Civil Española—the Spanish Civil War—ensued. The Spanish Republican freedom fighters implored the United States and President Franklin Delano Roosevelt for assistance, munitions and anything that would help them combat the usurping nationalist forces, but America officially ignored them. Consequently, liberals, progressives, anarchists and communists came from all over the world to take part in the defense of the Spanish Republic. But the fascists were backed and armed by Adolf Hitler and Benito Mussolini.

The conflict proved to be an excellent testing ground for the German and Italian military equipment and tactics that Hitler and Mussolini would bring to bear in Europe and Africa at the dawn of World War II. Needless to say, the good guys lost, and the leader of the fascist insurrection, General Francisco Franco, ruled Spain as a dictator until his death in 1975.

Not surprisingly, many Texans joined the fight. Fort Worth native Theodore Gibbs—a Black man who ran away from his home in Cowtown at the age of thirteen after witnessing the rape of his mother by her white employer—joined the freedom fighters in Spain and drove an ambulance until he was killed by an artillery shell. Conroe native Philip Detro rose to the rank of commander of the Lincoln-Washington Battalion of the International Brigade and led the scrappy contingent until succumbing to complications resulting from a sniper's bullet.[16] Laredo native Virgilio Gonzalez Davila served with the Washington Battalion and then transferred to the Forty-Sixth Division Campesinos, a "shock force" that fought in every major conflict of the war. And Texarkana native Samuel Conlon Nancarrow emigrated to Mexico after serving with the Peoples' Army of the Spanish Republic and went on to become one of the most original, influential musical composers of the twentieth century.

Benito Mussolini and Adolf Hitler were allies of the fascist side led by Francisco Franco in the Spanish Civil War. *Public domain*.

Spanish poet, playwright and theater director Federico García Lorca (*right*), pictured here with a young Salvador Dali, was executed by Spanish fascists for his liberal views in 1936. *Public domain.*

Oliver Law, a native of Matagorda, Texas, made history when he became the first African American to command an integrated military force in American history (though on Spanish soil). He was killed in action while leading the Abraham Lincoln Battalion in the first days of the Battle of Brunete.

Dozens of brave red-blooded Texas freedom fighters fought in Spain, serving alongside or hobnobbing with the likes of Ernest Hemingway, George Orwell, Langston Hughes, Pablo Neruda, Emma Goldman, Federico García Lorca, Paul Robeson, André Malraux and John Dos Passos. Unfortunately, they weren't the only Texans or, more precisely, Texas entities involved in the conflict.

A Texas firm chipped in as well. In 1902, an oil and gas venture—originally known as the Texas Company—was founded in Sour Lake, Texas, by oilman Joseph S. Cullinan and New York investor Arnold Schlaet. They formed the concern from the earlier Texas Fuel Company (in Beaumont), which had made a fortune acquiring and shipping oil from the legendary Spindletop oil field. The new incarnation was authorized to engage in the "storage and transportation of mineral solutions." According to the Texas State Historical Association online *Handbook of Texas*:

> *On May 1 the Texas Fuel Company conveyed its assets to the new company and was dissolved shortly afterward. The Texas Company was initially capitalized at $3 million and almost immediately began expanding operations. It used subsidiary companies for oil production and began acquiring barges and rail tank cars. It quickly covered new fields with leases. High production levels at two fields just outside Houston, the Sour Lake oilfield (1903) and the Humble oilfield (1905), provided the company with a secure financial base. In 1905 the Texas Company linked these two fields by pipelines to Port Arthur, ninety miles away, and built its first refinery there. That same year the company acquired an asphalt refinery*

at nearby Port Neches. In 1908 the company completed the ambitious venture of a pipeline from the Glenn Pool, in the Indian Territory (now Oklahoma), to its Southeast Texas refineries.

As early as 1905 the Texas Company had established marketing facilities not only throughout the United States, but also in Belgium, Luxembourg, and Panama. By 1911 the company had a presence in Mexico and Africa. In 1908 it moved its general offices from Beaumont to Houston, where they remained until autumn 1913. That year Cullinan was succeeded by Elgood C. Lufkin as president, and top-level management relocated to its New York offices, established at the company's founding by financier Arnold Schlaet. After World War I, the Texas Company developed and patented the Holmes-Manley refining process, the first continuous process for refining crude oil, which significantly increased the yield of gasoline from each barrel. The company expanded operations by establishing a refinery and two topping (or distillation) plants at Tanpilo, building three asphalt plants on the East Coast, and acquiring a refinery in Casper, Wyoming. On August 26, 1926, the company chartered a holding company in Delaware, the Texas Corporation, with capital of $250 million. In January 1927 the Texas Company also was chartered in Delaware as an operating company. At this time the Texas Company operated refineries in six Texas cities. Within a few years the company had added operating plants in Illinois, Wyoming, Colorado, Kentucky, California, and Montana and refineries in Bordeaux,

Spanish Civil War freedom fighter George Orwell would go on to author the dystopian masterpiece 1984. Wikipedia Commons.

France; Terdonck, Belgium; and Lethbridge, Alberta, Canada. In 1926 the pipeline system in the United States had reached 1,800 miles. With the acquisition of California Petroleum Corporation in 1928, the Texas Company became the first oil company to market refined products in then all forty-eight states. From 1929 to 1934, during the Great Depression, the company was operating at a loss and shut down some refineries. But its recovery was rapid as it expanded its international activities. In 1936 the Texas Company established exploration and production interests in the Middle East through a joint venture with Standard Oil Company of California (now Chevron). Other joint ventures consummated in 1936 included Caltex Petroleum Corporation, founded through consolidation of the Texas Company's marketing facilities east of Suez *with the producing and refining interests of Chevron on Bahrain Island in the Middle East, and P.T. Caltex Pacific Indonesia, a company holding concessions in Sumatra and Java. Today, both CPC and CPI remain among the world's most successful joint ventures.*

From there, the TSHA handbook entry jumps to how the Texas Company "significantly aided the American war effort" in World War II, which is obviously important. But what's arguably more important is what the entry leaves out.

In 1935, the Texas Company reached agreements to ship oil to the sitting liberal Spanish government. When the civil war started, however, the Texas Company refused to sell oil to the freedom fighters but allowed the conservative insurrectionists in Spain to put all the oil they imported (to operate and transport the German and Italian war machinery) on a tab until the conflict was over.

Rieber's "horse sense" told him it was much easier to deal with a tyrant than rabble guided by a representative government. In fact, as one friend put it, Rieber "always thought it was much better to deal with autocrats than democracies. He said with an autocrat you really only have to bribe them once. With democracies you have to keep doing it over and over."[17]

Torkild and the Texas Company didn't just fuel Franco, the Spanish fascists and, by extension, the Führer, however. They also used Texas Company oil freighters to spy for them. Which means the company profited from and ensured the victory of the bad guys before they profited from and ensured the victory of the good guys (in World War II) against the bad guys they had previously supported.

And the Texas Company threw its weight around to head this bad press off at the proverbial pass. In July 1940, *Life* magazine ran a handsome, celebratory feature on "'Cap' Rieber," lauding him for coming off a tanker "to build an oil empire and prove that industrial daring is not dead" and describing Torkild as the "most forthright, dynamic, hell-for-leather tycoon now operating in

After leading the Harlem Renaissance in New York, poet, social activist, novelist and playwright Langston Hughes supported the freedom fighters in the Spanish Civil War. *Wikipedia Commons.*

Six-foot, four-inch Conroe, Texas native Philip Detro rose to the rank of commander of the Lincoln-Washington Battalion in the Spanish Civil War. *Courtesy of the Abraham Lincoln Brigade Archives.*

the U.S."[18] The PR spread even included photos of Rieber at the White House, standing with a former Hollywood celebrity and holding a little indigenous Venezuelan boy while a Texas Company employee serviced oil pipeline equipment.[19] The eight-page campaign claimed that Rieber was a descendant of "Vitus Bering, the Danish explorer who discovered the Bering Strait in 1730," and concluded, "The nation needs able, hardboiled, daring business leaders—in short, Riebers."

The good press was effective, if often exaggerated, but Rieber admired Hitler and was still wheeling and dealing with the Nazis as late as August 1, 1941. When the truth came out, Rieber was forced to resign as leader of the Texas Company.

The company emerged from the entire treasonous fiasco virtually unscathed.

THIS IS PROBABLY THE point where I should not mention that the last two major military conflicts the United States has engaged in have largely been about oil. Instead, I'll just point out that the Texas Company is still around today. It is known to the general public as Texaco.

I should probably also not mention that, as you read these lines, it's actually against the law to protest an oil pipeline running through your backyard in Texas. And I shouldn't mention that oil and gas companies—like Texaco, now owned by Chevron—are still basically beholden to no one and still profit from mercenary opportunism and bullying, especially here, where "Big Oil" got its start.

3

IT'S A WONDERFUL LIE

Maybe I shouldn't be going on at such length about this, but I just can't get over the basic, utter inhumanity of it. She was either killed because she didn't put out, or because her life was less than the inconvenience of reporting a theft of $150.00. No matter which way you look at it, that's the value the Great Republican State of Texas placed on this Latina's life.
Don't get me wrong, I'm grateful that at least the guy was prosecuted…but seriously, Texas, what would Jesus say?
—J. Bearlaw, Daily Kos, 2013

You won't find many pictures of Lenora Ivie Frago, even on the internet. It's mostly the same photo of an attractive young woman of perhaps Hispanic descent. The image is incredibly grainy but still suggestive of beauty—beauty that's unfocused, unnoticed and forgotten. And that's definitely the case.

Frago has slipped our minds, intentionally or conveniently. She doesn't fit our narrative. Her death is an affront to our ideals and hypocrisy. Oh, and she's also actually Native American. And we definitely don't like to go there, unless Kevin Costner or Daniel Day-Lewis provides us with "White Savior" magnanimity. It's not how "true" stories play out in Texas.

During the wee hours of Christmas Eve 2009, twenty-seven-year-old San Antonio resident Ezekiel "Zeke" Gilbert decided he wanted to play *It's a Wonderful Life* via an escort service on Craigslist. He contacted the E-Street Girls Inc. "hotline" and made an appointment to "lasso the moon" in his Camino Real apartment in the 12200 block of Blanco Road.

At approximately 3:45 a.m., a twenty-three-year-old single mother of one, Frago, transported by her manager, Christopher "Topher" Perkins, showed up at Gilbert's door. Perkins waited in his car.

Gilbert paid $150 for thirty minutes of Frago's time, and he chatted her up before attempting to consummate what was no doubt his idea of a Christmas miracle. But something went awry. Gilbert wanted sex, but the original fee didn't include sex or whatever special kind of attention he felt he was due. Gilbert and Frago disagreed, and Frago decided to leave. Maybe it was a grift perpetrated by Perkins and Frago, but later, Gilbert never indicated as much to investigating detectives. Perhaps Frago didn't feel safe (Gilbert's gringo machismo was noted during his trial), or maybe Gilbert simply made Frago's skin crawl. It's even possible that Frago pressed Gilbert for more money for whatever might improve his Christmas spirits. It was hardly a G-rated transaction.

Henry Potter (Lionel Barrymore) in the 1946 Christmas classic *It's A Wonderful Life*. These days, Mr. Potters run Texas. *Wikipedia Commons*.

The dispute resulted in Frago's exit of Gilbert's apartment without him having experienced anything approaching *It's a Wonderful Life*, and he wasn't very happy. In fact, Gilbert got all Mr. Potter[20] about forfeiting his ill-conceived investment to procure illicit pleasures and confronted Perkins, a former nightclub bouncer. The conversation didn't go Gilbert's way, and Perkins and Frago started to leave. Then Gilbert did what so many other white Texan versions of Mr. Potter do when they feel they haven't been treated like the belle of the ball.

Gilbert moseyed over to his BMW and grabbed his AK-47.

If Frago was going to abandon him after he got hard, someone was—you guessed it—going to die hard. (Frago may not have known that allusion, because she was only two years old when *Die Hard*, another "Christmas" classic, came out.)

When Frago and Perkins got in the car, Frago screamed, "He's got a gun! Go! Go! Go!"[21]

Perkins pressed the proverbial pedal to the metal, but it didn't get them out of range soon enough. Gilbert fired two shots; one hit Perkins's car and ricocheted, lodging in the back of Frago's neck. She was paralyzed and died in a hospital several months later.

Gilbert was charged with aggravated assault until Frago died. Then he faced murder charges, and his case went to trial two and a half years later. His lawyers, Bobby Barrera and father Roy Barrera Sr., argued that Gilbert was simply trying to prevent the commission of a crime (theft), even though the property that he alleged was stolen ($150) was handed freely to the victim to make her an accomplice to another crime, according to Texas Penal Code 43.02: prostitution.[22]

The Barreras' defense of Gilbert's murder of Frago while attempting to commit the offense of soliciting prostitution was inane but very clever. In his opening statements, the junior Barrera said Frago "was there to rip" Gilbert off and that Gilbert had fired only to shoot out the tires of Perkins's vehicle. Then the Barreras dusted off a fifty-year-old statute—Texas Penal Code 9.42, deadly force to protect property—to trump their defendant's violation of 43.02. Essentially, 9.42 states that a person can utilize deadly force against another to protect land or property, especially when it is immediately necessary and, in particular, at nighttime and specifically if the land or property cannot be protected by any other means or if it would expose the would-be protector (or, in Gilbert's case, recoverer) to serious bodily harm or death.[23]

The ploy was an asinine farce, but the Barreras managed to keep straight faces, Gilbert feigned innocence and the jury was extraordinarily gullible or favorably predisposed. Gilbert's eventual "not guilty" verdict was an unflinching triumph of sexism, racism and classism, all at the same time. But no one—except almost everyone outside of Texas—seemed to notice. After all, our entire border with Mexico had been treated like a whorehouse for over one hundred years and well into the twentieth century. How dare Frago reject Gilbert's advances, especially after Gilbert paid $150 to get what so many typical Texans' grandfathers got for three pesos in the good ol' days.

HOW COULD SOMETHING LIKE this happen, you ask?

Your quandary and disbelief were echoed across the country. The webzine Above the Law put it bluntly, stating that Gilbert got "off on a technicality—the technicality in this case being that he didn't get off," and the jury ruled he could get away with killing Frago because she didn't get him off.

The Huffington Post headline read, "Ezekiel Gilbert Acquitted of Murdering Woman Who Wouldn't Have Sex." Gawker's headline said, "Texas Says It's OK to Shoot an Escort if She Won't Have Sex with You." The *Dallas Observer* headline read, "Sex Workers Pissed Off, Frightened by Acquittal of a San Antonio Man Who Killed an Escort."[24] And even Guns. com expressed or bragged about the sheer outrageousness of the decision: "Man Acquitted of Killing Hooker Who Would Not Give Him Sex."

An article in Tits and Sass, a website devoted to "service journalism by and for sex workers," suggested the Gilbert acquittal had broader implications:

> *This precedent is exceptionally deadly for women, both in the sex industry and not. Sex workers who feel uncomfortable when arriving to see a client and choose to not have sex with him have the threat of legally sanctioned death hanging over their head. But this can expand past that. Imagine the woman who answers a vague house cleaning post, babysitting post, or secretary post (all jobs I've seen listed on Craigslist that have carried an insinuation that sex was expected) and the man hiring her decides that sex is a mandatory part of the position. Her options now are: 1.) have sex she does not want to have, 2.) not be paid for her time/work, or 3.) get shot.*

Most of the headlines passively suggested that members of the jury were mouth-breathing cretins, and legendary journalist Kurt Eichenwald—who was educated at St. Mark's in Dallas—perfectly illustrated this notion by exploring the absurdity of Texas Penal Code Sec. 9.42 itself in a June 7, 2013 piece in *Vanity Fair*:

> *Under Texas law, if I see some kid getting ready to spray-paint his name on an underpass after dark, I can kill him. Criminal mischief at night can be a Class C misdemeanor involving less than $50 in damages, but in Texas, it effectively carries the death penalty. (Unless—and I can say this for damn sure—the youngster is a wealthy white boy. Then the murder charges will come raining down.) The enraged shooter can also kill anyone fleeing with a piece of property that isn't his.*
>
> *Still, Gilbert's case seems ridiculous. Essentially, he is claiming that he is able to compel the commission of a crime—prostitution—if he simply believed he was paying for sex or demand his money back for the service he was promised and did receive. (On the other hand, the cops testified in the case that Gilbert never suggested he was stopping a theft of his money.)*
>
> *Think of the possibilities. A guy buys some pot from a drug dealer, but it turns out to be oregano. If the drug dealer attempts to drive away—at night, of course—the purchaser can kill him. Or suppose someone buys something for what is advertised as the best price in town, later finds a lower one, goes back to the store manager, demands his money back, and is refused. Can the buyer then legally shoot the manager as he heads home that night? I don't see why not—at least that transaction involved a dispute about a legal transaction, rather than the crime Gilbert wanted performed.*

This section of the penal code—which implicitly permits individuals to stand their ground while engaging in criminal activity—is stupefying. Even presiding judge Mary Roman alluded to this point after the verdict. "It needs to be amended," she said. "It was just unfortunate. I don't believe that was the legislative intent at all."[25]

Is she right?

Well, Gilbert obviously believed he was "dispossessed" of his cash and of the act of prostitution he assumed said funds would purchase. But this isn't quantum physics. There was no evidence that Frago perpetuated this "dispossession by using force, threat, or fraud against the actor." In the police interview conducted with Gilbert after the incident, as homicide detective Raymond Roberts told the court, Gilbert "never mentioned anything about theft."

Regarding Gilbert's determination that deadly force was immediately necessary, couldn't he simply have called the police and given them the make and model of the car and maybe even the license plate number? Isn't that a reasonable assumption that might make a demonstration of potentially deadly force irresponsible if not criminal?

Oh, right.

If Gilbert had called the police, he obviously would have incriminated himself.

Unquestionably, however, nighttime is the right time, and that was where the Barreras really earned their angels' wings. It was "nighttime"—4:15 a.m., to be exact—and Gilbert clearly considered Frago's Grinch-like rejection of his version of *It's a Wonderful Life* a theft of sorts, and she did abscond with the cash he believed would secure it.

Call me crazy, but is firing an assault rifle at someone's car over $150 reasonable, and is $150 in any way, shape or form worth risking killing someone over, even if you have no recourse or means of replenishing the kitty for future escapades in the skin trade?

Shouldn't Gilbert simply have done what most other lonely, horny gun nuts in this state do? Masturbate in their favorite recliner while thinking about escorts or staring lovingly at their semiautomatic rifles?

THE BULLET THAT LODGED in Frago's neck left her bedridden and dependent on a respirator. Some months after, the respirator became disconnected, and the resulting deprival of steady oxygen left her brain damaged, never to recover. Frago was taken off life support in July 2010.

The shameless Barreras argued that Frago's delayed death wasn't Gilbert's fault, but neurologist Augusto Parra disagreed. "When you are bedridden like" Frago, Parra stated, "with mechanical support, with tubes for feeding… these patients are prone to have complications. She was in this situation because she was shot."

During the trial, Gilbert was on his best behavior and cleaned up pretty well for the proceedings. It was a far cry from Perkins's description of him the night he shot Frago. "His whole posture was about him trying to appear bigger than he was," Perkins testified, indicating that Gilbert's face was "stone cold" and that he comported himself with a kind of "gangster swagger."[26]

The San Antonio jurors who weighed in on Gilbert's guilt or innocence for eleven hours over two days, however, saw through the facts, looked past the tragic death of an unfortunate or perhaps imperfect single mother and crowned the white guy innocent. It's a common Texas theme, but Gilbert earned it. He put on a command performance. He hugged the Barreras and confirmed the bamboozled jury's intuitions. He thanked God, his attorneys and the jury for seeing "what wasn't the truth" and giving him a "second chance." But he didn't stop there.

"I sincerely regret the loss of life of Miss Frago," he said. "I've been in a mental prison the past four years of my life. I have nightmares. If I see guns on TV where people are getting killed, I change the channel."[27]

Not so coincidentally, I think I've been in a "mental prison" ever since this bizarre miscarriage of justice. Back in those days, we didn't have semiautomatic slaughters every other month. It was fairly new, but I guess it foreshadowed things to come.

I RECENTLY REACHED OUT to two of the most prominent members of the prosecutorial team. One never returned my call, and the other said they didn't know if their current employer would approve of them commenting on the trial—they said they would check but never called back. I also reached out to one of Frago's brothers. He had cared for his sister while she was in the hospital and was heartbroken when she died and crushed when Gilbert was acquitted. I didn't get to talk to him, but I did speak with his wife. She told me her husband finished raising Frago's daughter and told her to tell me that he didn't want to talk about it, presumably because he wasn't up to revisiting the entire nightmare again.

But I fear it's too late for that. To suggest that the Barreras and Gilbert perpetrated a Texas-sized line of bullpucky of the highest magnitude isn't enough.

A little less than a year before Gilbert's trial, the bond company that posted his $250,000 bail asked to be released from their contract on the bond because Gilbert was living in Las Vegas and frequently changing his cellphone numbers. The bond firm was receiving reports that he intended to jump bail.[28] In fact, bounty hunters were eventually enlisted to bring him back to stand trial.[29] And now, just ten years after the declaration of Gilbert's innocence, here's the sickening punchline.

After an Alamo City jury acquitted Gilbert, he returned to Las Vegas and used his second chance to resume his posture of "gangster swagger." He's had run-ins with the law involving drugs and domestic battery and, in early September 2017, for using Snapchat to recruit a young woman into prostitution. Gilbert's girlfriend, twenty-year-old Wynter Nicole Fowler, sent the woman pictures of Rolex watches, Versace purses and a Rolls-Royce, along with claims of earning thousands of dollars in Sin City.

Mug shots after Ezekiel Gilbert demanded prostitution in 2009 and was caught sex-trafficking in 2017. *Public domain.*

The gullible woman fell for Gilbert and Fowler's pitch and relocated to Vegas, where she was soon working as a prostitute for Gilbert. About a month into her "employment," however, she decided to quit. Gilbert threatened her and boasted that he'd already "gotten away with murder" in Texas.

On September 12, 2017, Gilbert and Fowler were arrested and booked on charges of sex trafficking and conspiracy to commit sex trafficking. When police searched Gilbert's residence, they found several guns and more than $400,000 in cash.

Gilbert and Fowler both worked with investigators and received plea deals that reduced the charges against them and mitigated their sentences. And, even better, Gilbert had clearly liberated himself from his "mental prison" and mastered his fear of guns. His Las Vegas attorney portrayed him as a repentant, hardworking average Joe recently diagnosed with cancer and dabbling in servicing Johns only as a desperate side hustle. Gilbert delivered another command performance, informing the judge that he fully accepted responsibility for his actions. "I'm sorry and I just wish, if granted, I could live life and continue with my credit repair and take care of my health."[30]

Gilbert was sentenced to probation and twelve weekends in jail, so that he could still work and seek treatment for his malady. He obviously had a guardian angel. Perhaps he got his "wonderful life" after all.

HE DOESN'T WANT TO talk about it, one way or another—because I called him in early December 2022.

When a man answered the phone, he said he was not Ezekiel Gilbert and said the phone no longer belonged to him but that he could take a message. He asked me my name, and I gave it. Then he asked me what the call was about.

"I wanted to talk to [Gilbert] about a case he was involved in here in Texas a while back," I said.

"Oh," he replied. "What kind of case? Are you a police officer? I'm sorry. I'm trying to write down notes."

"No," I said. "I'm a writer. I'm writing about the death of Lenora Frago."

"Oh, OK," the man replied. "This isn't his number anymore. He actually called me a while back and said I could take messages for important stuff or whatever. I reckon this is important....I can give him the message and have him give you a holler back. This is 'Mills'?"

"Bills," I corrected. "B-I-L-L-S. I was wondering if I could get his side of the story. Obviously, I'm aware of his legal issues in Las Vegas, which mirror in some ways some of the stuff that went on in Texas and don't lend credence to his original acquittal, so I just wanted his opinion. I mean, I heard he has cancer or was being treated for cancer, and sometimes people become repentant or they remember things differently...or look at things differently. Sometimes, they don't."

There was a long pause, so I said, "So give him my message."

"Pardon me?" the man said.

"So give him my message," I repeated.

"You should ask a little nicer than that," he replied. "Lose this fucking number, homeboy."

I DIDN'T LOSE GILBERT'S number.

I actually thought about giving it to Patrick Crusius, the Dallas man who drove from Big D to El Paso on August 3, 2019, to gun down twenty-three Mexican Americans with a semiautomatic civilian version of the AK-47. Maybe Gilbert could be an expert witness on protecting one's property—which, in Crusius's case, could be argued was all of Texas. White men are being told by Fox News, Alex Jones types and 2020 election loser Donald J. Trump that they're being dispossessed. Maybe Gilbert could even do a photo op with the Barreras, fearless gun rights advocate Governor Greg Abbott and Texas transplant Kyle Rittenhouse.

Today, Lenora Ivie Frago is almost entirely forgotten in San Antonio and Texas, and her outrageous murder and Gilbert's preposterous acquittal aren't on anyone's radar. Had Frago received Gilbert's second or third chance, she would have been thirty-six this past Christmas Eve, and she may have gotten to spend it with her daughter, who is grown now.

But again, that's not how true stories play out in Texas.

We all know there will be more guns than books under Lone Star Christmas trees this year. And more El Paso Walmarts, Santa Fe high schools, Uvalde elementary schools and other gun massacres in the months to come. Because in the Lone Star version of *It's a Wonderful Life*—though our Mr. Potter is also a wheelchair-bound reprobate—Christmas is a wonderful lie.

So, images of victims like Frago will continue to fade, appear grainy and recede in our collective memory.

4

THE CART WAR

*I do not think there was ever a more wicked war than that waged by the United
States on Mexico. I thought so at the time, when I was a youngster, only I had
not moral courage enough to resign. I had taken an oath to serve eight years, unless
sooner discharged, and I considered my supreme duty was to my flag.
I had a horror of the Mexican War, and I have always believed that it was on
our part most unjust. The wickedness was not in the way our soldiers conducted
it, but in the conduct of our government in declaring war. The troops behaved well
in Mexico, and the government acted handsomely about the peace.
We had no claim on Mexico. Texas had no claim beyond the Nueces River,
and yet we pushed on to the Rio Grande and crossed it. I am always ashamed of
my country when I think of that invasion.*
—Ulysses S. Grant, from *A Tour Around the World by General Grant*
(1879)

American president Ulysses S. Grant was no lightweight, and his
remorse, noted above, cannot be ignored. He states it plain. The
Texas Revolution (October 2, 1835–April 21, 1836), a rebellion
of colonists from the United States and Tejanos (Hispanic Texans) against
the government of Mexico—the intent of which is still hotly debated even
today—was one thing. The Mexican-American War, known in Mexico as
the *Intervención Estadounidense en México* (United States intervention in Mexico),
which followed the 1845 American annexation of Texas (which Mexico still
considered its territory), was quite another.

The former has lost much of its sheen, and the latter, as Grant quite earnestly conveys, arguably never had any to begin with. And each later contributed in its way to Texas's role in the American Civil War. But there was another "war" after the first two and before the Civil War—it just reflects so badly on Anglo-Americans (white Texans) that it's basically ignored today.

ON THE WAY BACK from Corpus Christi in late July 2018, I drove through Goliad for the first time. Sometimes, I take different routes in order to explore or just flit around, maybe loaf a little. I was immediately struck by an incredible tree on the north side of the Goliad County Courthouse, between Commercial and Market Streets. I parked, took some pictures and sat on a bench. I liked the tree. I liked the dramatic appearance of the Goliad County Courthouse through the branches of the tree. I spotted a stone-mounted historical marker and examined it. Erected in 1964, the marker, for "The Hanging Tree," gave me a short history lesson.

> *Site for court sessions at various times from 1846 to 1870. Capital sentences called for by the courts were carried out immediately, by means of a rope and a convenient limb.*
>
> *Hangings not called for by regular courts occurred here during the 1857 "Cart War"—a series of attacks made by Texas freighters against Mexican drivers along the Indianola–Goliad–San Antonio Road. About 70 men were killed, some of them on this tree, before the war was halted by Texas Rangers.*

"Hangings not called for by regular courts." Lynchings.

The tree, which I later learned was also referred to as the Cart War Oak, suddenly seemed Lovecraftian.

Here is the Texas State Historical Association *Handbook of Texas* citation's first paragraph on the "Cart War":

> *The so called "Cart War" erupted in 1857 and had national and international repercussions. The underlying causes of the event, historians believe, were ethnic and racial hostilities of Texans toward Mexican Texans, exacerbated by the ethnocentrism of the Know-Nothing party and the White anger over Mexican sympathy with Black slaves. By the mid-1850s, Mexicans and Tejanos had built a successful business of hauling food and merchandise from the port of Indianola[31] to San Antonio and other*

The Cart War Oak "Hanging Tree" still stands on the Goliad County Courthouse lawn in Goliad, Texas. *Photo by author.*

> *towns in the interior of Texas. Using oxcarts, Mexicans moved freight more rapidly and cheaply than their Anglo competitors. Some Anglos retaliated by destroying the Mexicans' oxcarts, stealing their freight, and reportedly killing and wounding a number of Mexican carters.*[32]

Mexican Americans and Hispanic immigrants taking Anglo Texans' jobs. Ethnocentrism, as in Anglocentrism. And an angry, "Know-Nothing" faction in our government that didn't know much or care about knowing much.

It sounded familiar.

The local authorities made no serious effort to apprehend the perpetrators of violence against the Mexican American and Mexican teamsters, much less punish them for their transgressions. And the September 24, 1857 edition of the *San Antonio Texan* wasn't having it:

> *These Mexicans are citizens of Texas, they were born here, and they or their fathers fought against Mexico for that liberty they now enjoy— "liberty," did we say—rather a poor show for liberty when they are not allowed to*

63

pursue their daily labor without being shot down like dogs! And for no other excuse than because they live cheap.

Hardly disproving the *Texan*'s charge, the September 26, 1857 edition of the *Weekly Independent* in Belton countered it disapprovingly:

From a gentleman of our acquaintance, who has for something more than a year past been a citizen of San Antonio, we learn that this war has not been waged against Mexican cartmen on account of the difference in the prices they charge for hauling, nor is it believed that other Wagoners are the only ones who attack them, but it is on account of the thieving of those greaser wagoners or cart-men on the road.

On September 12, 1857, seventeen Mexican oxcarts were attacked by thirty to forty men near Helena in Karnes County. The attackers' faces were "either masked or blackened,"[33] and the men murdered Jose Antonio Delgado. Some reports indicate that he had been shot fourteen times. Esteban, Martinio and Nicandr Valdez were wounded. Delgado was a prominent San Antonio citizen who had served under Andrew Jackson in the Battle of New Orleans in the War of 1812 and was a respected veteran of the Texas Revolution.

Texas governor Elisha Marshall Pease subsequently issued a $500 reward for the arrest of any member of the attacking party[34] and urged law enforcement personnel to remain vigilant and apprehend the perpetrators.

Some accounts suggest that a significant percentage of the trouble occurred around Goliad, and some reports indicate that several Mexican American oxcart drivers were hanged from the namesake Cart War Oak on the courthouse lawn. The irony, of course, was that Texans of Anglo and Mexican descent had gathered in Goliad in 1835 to sign the Texas Declaration of Independence, and only two signatories were native Texians—José Francisco Ruiz and José Antonio Navarro. All the rest were immigrants from somewhere else—Anglo immigrants.

As the violence continued to escalate, Mexican minister Manuel Robles y Pezuela protested the bloodshed to Secretary of State Lewis Cass,[35] who, in turn, urged Governor Pease[36] to take action. On November 30, 1857, Pease addressed the Texas legislature and requested a special appropriation.

Gentlemen of the Senate and House of Representatives
Information has been received at this office, that a train of carts, from San Antonio to the Coast, driven by Mexicans, and under the charge of

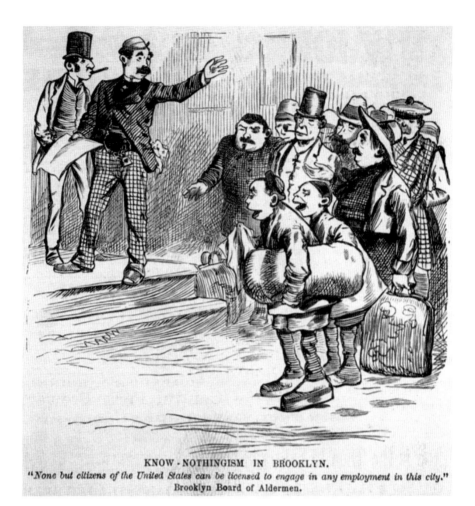

KNOW - NOTHINGISM IN BROOKLYN.
"*None but citizens of the United States can be licensed to engage in any employment in this city.*"
Brooklyn Board of Aldermen.

Constituents of the Know-Nothing Party weren't fans of immigrants in the North or South, but some eventually came around. *Wikipedia Commons.*

Mr. Wm. Pyron, an American, encamped on the night of the 20th inst, on Yates Creek, the next morning while the Mexicans were getting up their oxen. They were assaulted and fired upon by a party of armed men, and two of them were killed.

No blame whatever attaches to Capt. Nelson or the company under his command, as Mr. Pyron did not apply to them for an escort. It is understood that he preferred to go without an escort, in consequence of assurances of safety that had been given him by parties in Karnes and Goliad Counties, he having previously made a trip without molestation.

After this misfortune Mr. Pyron returned to the Cibolo, where Capt. Nelson's Company were encamped, and applied for and received an escort for his train.

It is painful to have to record such acts of violence, and a subject of deep mortification that the law places no means in my power to prevent them. Such outrages cannot occur and pass unpunished in a country where the Officers and the mass of the people entertain a proper respect for the laws. And it becomes a matter for your consideration, whether the citizens of a country that permits such acts to be done with impunity, should not be compelled to pay a heavy pecuniary penalty. This would, without doubt arouse them to the necessity of preserving the public peace.

It is now very evident that there is no security for the lives of citizens of Mexican origin engaged in the business of transportation along the road from San Antonio to the Gulf, unless they are escorted by a military force. The term of service of the Militia now employed will expire on the 8th day of December, and unless some direction is received from the Legislature to continue their services, I shall feel it my duty to discharge them on that day.

It will require an appropriation of about fourteen thousand and five hundred dollars[37] to pay the services of the Company, and for their subsistence and forage.

On the approval of the appropriation and the deployment of armed escorts, the Cart War ended in December 1857. But there were Anglo grumblings until the end. A commentary in the December 5, 1857 edition of the *Belton Weekly Independent* was chilling and remorseless: "That there were some Mexicans killed no one denies, but that as many were killed as ought to be, we believe no one will admit."

On Saturday, January 23, 1858, the *Colorado Citizen* of Columbus, Texas, "remonstrated against" Pease's action and held forth in a classless (or class-minded), racist manner:

That the citizens of Goliad and Karnes have been harassed to death by contemptible Mexican greasers or peons, we have not a doubt. We respect a decent Mexican citizen, but for these low, thieving Mexican peons, we have no sympathy—they are not deserving of it. We remember that about two years ago some of them were driven out of Caldwell County by citizens for tampering with slaves, and inducing them to run off to Mexico; and in the summer of '56, during the inchoated negro insurrection in this county, some five or six Mexicans were implicated in the insurrection and banished by our

President Ulysses S. Grant believed that the U.S. intervention into (and annexation of) Mexican territory in Texas after the Mexican-American War was "wicked." *Wikipedia Commons.*

citizens. Some of these Mexicans had negro wives and placed themselves on an equality with the negroes.

The truth is this class of Mexicans are no better than negroes and we had as soon go to the polls and vote with a free negro. We do not say this in disparagement of the more respectable class of Mexican citizens; for we are aware that there are such, and as such they are entitled to the same respect and privileges that American citizens are. We do not know, but it seems to us it would have been more proper and wise in the Governor to have let alone the matter and left the citizens of Goliad and Karnes to settle the difficulty themselves. We doubt not there are enough good, law-abiding citizens in these counties to insure [sic] justice to all parties, and to deal with the Mexican greasers or peons—who, it appears, from the testimony of our correspondent, are connected with abolitionist associations, and are running off slaves into Mexico—in accordance with true patriotism and the spirit of our institutions.

This opinion was not isolated.

Image of a Mexican oxcart, which Mexicans and Mexican Americans used to compete against Anglo-American drovers. *Courtesy of DeGolyer Library, Southern Methodist University.*

The majority of white Texans of the period had come to consider their Mexican and Mexican American neighbors "as racially inferior, culturally defective, and morally corrupt."[38] And actually, two years before the Cart War officially commenced, the Austin-based *Texas Gazette* printed a prescient story titled "Worthy of Notice."

> *A Writer in the San Antonio Ledger suggests that every Peon Mexican coming to San Antonio be compelled to register his name at the Mayor's office, and give an account of himself and his business; that, also, if he is unknown to any respectable resident of San Antonio, and unable to give a satisfactory certificate, that he be required under penalty of law to leave the city forthwith. It is a most troublesome class in the community—one far more mischievous than free negroes, and they are doubtless all of them fugitives from service and labor in Mexico. Something of a stringent nature ought to be put in force against them. We may suffer the peon to stay among us who labors and shows himself to be honest and industrious, but we cannot permit the peons to increase in our community unrestrainedly without serious loss to citizens. It is a bad element of society, and sooner or later will be entirely extinguished.[39]*

In 2018, Utah State University professor Maria Diaz placed the entire situation in context: "The Cart War in Texas encapsulated a period in which the place of Mexican laborers—and, indeed, the Mexican people writ large—was defined by the limits of a white/black binary. In the aftermath of the U.S.-Mexican War more southerners migrated to Texas, slavery continued to take root, and Mexican Texans became entangled in a world not of their own making—one in which they were caught in between social classes and racial castes."[40]

THE CART WAR HAS been ignored of late, but such was not always the case.

In a *Texas Siftings*[41] piece reprinted in the July 18, 1885 edition of the *Palo Pinto Star*, the affair was far from forgotten. The story even discussed a fascinating warning "sign" that remained for years after the bloodshed.

> *One of those old-fashioned wooden wheels would be a curiosity nowadays in San Antonio. There is only one in the country, and it is up in a mesquite tree in Atascosa County. It got there in a very singular way.*
>
> *About 1856 the American teamsters, who competed with the Mexicans in transporting freight to San Antonio, discovered that they were being ruined by cheap Mexican labor. The San Antonio merchants preferred to have their goods brought from the coast by Mexican carelas, for the reason that the Mexicans were more reliable. They did not extract whisky from the barrels and fill them up with water, and help themselves generally to the goods entrusted to them, as did the Anglo-Saxon teamsters, whose go-ahead-ativeness could not be repressed.*
>
> *The result was "the Cart War," in which many Mexicans were killed, and their carelas burned. The old-fashioned wooden wheel, away up in a mesquite tree, marks the site of one of these fights. For some reason or another, the American teamsters stuck the wheel up in a tree, possibly as a warning to other Mexicans. A limb of the tree grew through the hole in the wheel, and today it looks very peculiar up on the tree to a stranger, who imagines that the tree grew up suddenly under the wagon, while it was passing, and tore a wheel off.*

In *A New History of Texas for Schools* by Anna J. Hardwicke Pennybacker of Palestine, Texas, the citation for the "Cart War" appears as follows:

> *At this time Mexican teamsters were doing most of the hauling from the sea-ports to San Antonio, for they worked more cheaply than Texas wagoners, and were quite as reliable. In spite of public warnings, farmers*

and merchants continued to employ the labor they could get for the least money. The Texas workmen then attacked the teams of Mexicans, stole their goods, killed their animals, destroyed their wagons, and, in some cases, murdered the drivers. Indignant at the cruel treatment inflicted upon his countrymen, the Mexican Minister (October, 1857) complained to the United States authorities. In November, Governor Pease sent two special messages bearing on this subject, to the Legislature, and finally, to protect the Mexicans, ordered out seventy-five militiamen, who, with the assistance of law-abiding citizens, restored order.[42]

Some might call the mention progress, but Pennybacker's textbook was published in 1895, and hardly anyone has heard of the Cart War today.

5

PREGNANT WITH DEATH

*Our country's national crime is lynching. It is not the creature of an hour,
the sudden outburst of uncontrolled fury, or the unspeakable brutality
of an insane mob.*
—Ida B. Wells, speech in Chicago, Illinois, January 1900

At approximately 3:00 a.m. on Saturday, July 20, 1895, a terrifying explosion occurred two miles southeast of Mart, Texas. Twenty miles east of Waco, and barely across the Falls County line, the sound of the explosion was heard from ten miles away, and the people of Mart dressed quickly and went out into the night to determine the origin of the blast.

Emmett and Prince Elliott and J.C. Douglass saw smoke and flames in the distance. They were reportedly the first to arrive at the scene of the carnage. They could scarcely believe their eyes. The debris radius was lit by human candles—human corpses on fire.

What had been a familiar house owned by a respected Black family was now a smoldering crater. A partially denuded Black woman was walking around with a baby cradled in her arms. A young, Black male hired hand was leaning against the remains of a structure, bloody and inarticulate. The bodies of Mary "Fanny" Phillips, her three sons—Tom, Absalom Jr. and William—and Hannah Williams, her granddaughter, were scattered across the area wrapped in flames that emitted an unspeakably grotesque light. Fanny's body was knotted up in her bedsprings, her knees touching her chin

SCENE AFTER THE EXPLOSION.

1. Where Fanny Phillips fell, wound up in bed springs. She was blown twenty-three yards and was burned, doubled up in the springs.

2. Hannah Williams, the young girl. She was blown twenty-six yards.

3. Tom Phillips, a boy. Was blown twenty yards.

4 and 5. Will and Ab Phillips, boys, were blown sixteen yards and fell ten yards apart.

6. Where Henry Hill's wife stood with their baby in her arms and saw her mother and brothers burning to death. She was slightly bruised and her baby was not hurt.

7. The direction old black Ben Harrison, bleeding, blind and crazed from the explosion, fled from the ruins.

8. Where Kid Taylor, a black negro about 20 years old leaned against the fence. His clothing was in tatters and he was bleeding and dizzy.

9. The spot where the cottage stood. It was covered all over with debris, such as broken stoves, tables, trunks, fire arms and masses of splinters.

10. The cyclone cellar which remained intact.

11. The farm wagon.

12. The smokehouse, which was destroyed.

13. The corn crib, thirty yards from the house. It was uninjured.

14. Elm trees in the yard, the boughs of which hung thick with wreckage.

15. The hole blown in the earth by the explosion.

Scene of a vengeful act of racial terror (involving dynamite) in Falls County in 1895. *Courtesy of the* Galveston Daily News.

and her entire figure "baked and shrunken." Fanny's brother Ben Harrison was found several hundred feet away, blinded, maimed, half-naked and "incoherently muttering."

Fanny, Tom, Absalom Jr., William Phillips and little Hannah Williams were "Blown to Eternity"[43] by a significant quantity of dynamite, and their white neighbors in Mart were shocked.

DURING A BREAK IN my writing schedule in 2017, I decided to pursue a story that had bothered me for a couple of years. It involved the aforementioned tragedy in Central Texas, but it was based on secondary and tertiary sources and seemed to have vanished from local histories.

Just because you go looking, however, doesn't mean you'll find anything. The past—which takes a long time to happen—takes even longer to sort out. It was a fishing expedition, and I didn't get a single bite. The incident (or series of incidents) was so old and buried it might as well have never happened.

Texas is funny like that.

I tried to pinpoint the exact location of the former Phillips place but had no luck. Then I stopped by the Nancy Nail Memorial Library in Mart and spoke with a white librarian and a white patron who had lived in the town for decades. I discussed the information I was seeking, and they seemed surprised. They had never heard of the explosion. In fact, they wanted copies of what I had so they could start a folder about it in the library. I obliged them, and the librarian gave me the name of the oldest living Black citizen in the community and said I should contact her. I did, but she was also entirely unfamiliar with the incident. She'd never heard anyone—Black or white—ever mention it.

It was one thing to go into a community and remind them of something that had happened because they had denied it happened or covered it up. This was obviously different, because Mart didn't have a reputation like Palestine or Slocum or even the nearby McLennan County seat, Waco, where two African Americans had been burned at the stake, one in front of a cheering crowd of thousands of white people (while the mayor and police chief watched) and chronicled in photographs that became popular lynching postcards.

Mart seemed like a nice town, and I was confronted with a community that wasn't actively engaged in conspicuous obfuscation. Would exposing a local atrocity improve race relations or make them worse? Would writing

Ida Bell Wells, investigative journalist, educator and early leader in the civil rights movement, was one of the founders of the NAACP. *Public domain.*

about this incident foster a kumbaya moment or create racial resentment where there seemed very little to speak of?

It was a conundrum.

I decided to err on the side of the truth—so far as it could be known.

As additional investigation revealed, the origin of the July 20, 1895 blast stemmed from an incident three months prior, on April 17. Here is a published account dated April 18, 1895, in the "Budget of News from Waco" section in the *Fort Worth Daily Gazette* the following day:

> *Further particulars and details of the tragedy near Mart yesterday evening have been received and show it to have been a most fatal one. Two men are dying and the third is fatally wounded. Phil, George and Ned Arnold, brothers, are young farmers living at and near the tragedy. It seems that Ned Arnold recently brought to the neighborhood several young negroes from Arkansas for farm work. At present he had no work for them and he had told his brother Phil that he might secure the negroes to work for him. One young negro of the party had become a friend of Abe Phillips, a negro*

farmer of the community, and the latter sought to prevent the lad from going to work for Phil Arnold. After several ineffectual attempts to secure his services, Phil and George Arnold and Watts Vaughn at noon yesterday went to Phillips' house to induce the negro to work.

They were unsuccessful and as they were leaving Phillips followed them. When about 600 yards from his house he was heard to say: "G—D yes, and I'll shoot you." He immediately opened fire on Phil Arnold with a revolver and had fired two shots without effect when Arnold brought his revolver into play and fired four times, putting as many bullets in the negro's body, one through the stomach and three in the head.

When Phillips opened fire Richard Bragg, a negro, in front of whose house the shooting occurred, began firing at Ned Arnold. The latter returned the fire and Bragg was shot in the wrist and through the bowels. His wound is fatal.

A few moments after Phil Arnold had shot Phillips the latter's son, Wes Phillips, a boy of 17 or 18 years of age, qietly [sic] walked up and emptied the contents of a double-barreled shotgun into Phil Arnold's back, killing him almost instantly.

The negro lad made his escape and he immediately sought the officers of the county [Falls County] *to give himself up, fearing lynching at the hands of Arnold's friends. He reached Reisel last night and was turned over to the sheriff of Falls County and jailed at Marlin.*

The community in the neighborhood of the tragedy is greatly excited and deplores the affair.

The Arnolds are said to be highly respected and peaceable young men, while the negro Phillips, who was killed, has always been considered a troublesome character.

Virgil Gillespie, a young farmer and neighbor of the Arnolds, arrived in [Waco] *this morning to purchase burial clothes for the body of Arnold and told the story of the tragedy to the reporter.*

It was the most detailed report I could find on the incident. The *Galveston Daily News* account of April 19 provided one more salient detail: "The trouble resulted from a bound boy who ran away from Arnold."

Bound boy. This was not a term I was familiar with, so I looked it up.

Obviously archaic, "bound boy" referred to someone who was often sent or taken from an orphanage to become an "indentured servant." This would primarily refer to a white child,[44] not a Black enslaved person or, arguably, even a recent descendant of slaves so soon after Reconstruction in

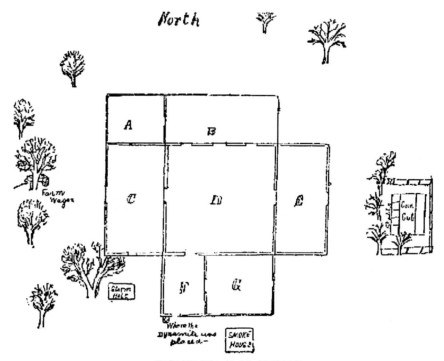

GROUND PLAN OF COTTAGE.

A. Room cut off by partition from the north gallery occupied by Ben Harrison and Kid Taylor, both of whom were badly hurt, but will recover.
B. Open gallery.
C. Shed room, west side of house, unoccupied.
D. Big room occupied by Fanny Phillips and her three sons, Ab, William and Tommy and Hannah Williams, her grand-daughter, all of whom were killed and roasted.
E. Shed room east side, occupied by Henry Hill and his wife and baby, who were blown out toward the corn crib and sustained slight injuries.
F. Kitchen under which the dynamite was placed.
G. Shed room partitioned from the kitchen, unoccupied.

Original floor plan of the Phillips cottage in Falls County (just south of Mart, Texas) before the explosion. *Courtesy of the* Galveston Daily News.

Arkansas, Texas or any other area in the former proslavery South. Slavery-like conditions still existed. Did Phil Arnold bring "bound" Black boys (or men) from Arkansas to work for him? Did Abe Phillips unintentionally or intentionally attempt to nullify this illicit and possible criminal agreement? Or did one of the Blacks Arnold brought down from Arkansas simply decide he no longer wanted to work for him? Texas wasn't a "right to work" state back then, any more than it is now—but it was much worse for African Americans. That's why so many migrated north.[45]

Whatever transpired to deliver three "bound" young Black men to the Mart area, Abe Phillips apparently complicated the agreed upon—or forced upon—terms. And the resulting confrontation was deadly.

ALMOST THREE MONTHS TO the day after the altercation, someone detonated explosives under Abe Wilson's widow's house.[46] It disturbed the Mart community.

Before the sun rose hundreds of people on the ground were gazing with awe at the horrible scene in which a household had been annihilated with dynamite in an explosion so terrific that doves, scissor tails and mocking birds roosting in the elms had not only been killed but picked clean of feathers, and a six-room cottage had been effaced and no fragment of it left too large to go into an average heating stove. Wherever one goes in the precinct, whatever group he joins, he finds the explosion under discussion. In the fertile valleys the crops are laid by and the affluent farmers have organized protracted meetings where eloquent ministers are administering spiritual pabulum to large congregations, but in the intervals the congregation scatter under the shade trees, turn their faces toward the Smith-Strange farm,[47] and talk about dynamite.[48]

Commenting on the local produce, a Black woman said that "things don't taste right 'round here" anymore. And the more superstitious elements of the African American community believed a "supernatural agency was involved." They claimed ghosts wandered among the elms and shrieked through the night in the rows of cotton.

On the evening after the Phillips house was destroyed, three Black men were fired upon when they attempted to retrieve a wagon, presumably to help clean up the destruction.

The people of Mart were indignant. And the curious onlookers did more than gather souvenirs. They helped treat the wounded, assisted in burying the dead and held a public meeting to condemn the atrocity, even drafting a resolution:

Whereas, a rapacious crime was committed in our community on the night of the 20th instant in the massacre of a family of negroes, some unoffending children being in their number, by the use of some explosive substance, causing the instantaneous death of five persons and seriously wounding two others, and the following night some negroes proceeding upon the public highway were fired upon, as we believe, with intent to kill, and

Whereas, such unlawful acts are calculated to tarnish the fair name of our community and thus deter good people from settling among us, be it

Resolved, that we citizens of Mart community, in mass meeting assembled, desire to express our total disapproval and condemnation of

South or back view, showing the smoke-house which was destroyed with the cottage. Near the forked elm tree the cyclone cellar roof is shown. The dynamite was placed under the kitchen, to the right of the corner block and perpendicularly beneath the tall stovepipe of the cooking stove.

Southerly rear view of the Phillips cottage in Falls County before the bombing. *Courtesy of the Galveston Daily News.*

such unlawful acts and deeply deplore their occurrence in our midst, and we invite and demand the fullest investigation of the affair by the proper authorities, and we promise any assistance that may be within our power to enable the officers to bring the criminals to justice.

Resolved, that a petition to the governor of the state, signed by the members of this meeting, be forwarded asking that a sufficient reward be offered to induce a first-class detective to penetrate the mystery that seems to surround this affair.[49]

In the days that followed, it was discovered that a child had died in the Phillips house on the Thursday before the explosion, and while the Phillips family was at the child's funeral in Harrison (eight miles north of Mart and eight miles southeast of Waco), the Phillip family's "watch dog" was poisoned. Then, after the explosion, which spread debris over seventy-five acres[50] and blew the Phillips smokehouse to smithereens, local dogs who partook of the scattered Phillips bacon store got sick, and some died. According to one local doctor, the "atmosphere around the Phillips premises was pregnant with death."

North ou front view of the Phillips cottage, showing the shed room on the left, which was occupied by Henry Hill and his wife and baby, this family being blown up and all escaping injury, except the wife, who was bruised on the leg. On the righthand end of the portico or gallery Gen. Harrison and Kid Taylor slept, both of whom were badly hurt.

Northerly front view of the Phillips residence before it was bombed in 1895. *Courtesy of the* Galveston Daily News.

The perpetrators of the atrocity didn't leave anything to chance. If there were any questions as to whether a white life mattered more than a Black life on July 20, 1895, the answer at the Phillips residence was resounding. And a local witness, again, described the ghastly carnage. "There they lay, scorched and burning, their eyes starting, grinning as if in horror, mutely detailing the story of an outrage which I hope will stand alone in the annals of Texas crime. I hope the man who did the deed saw his handiwork as I saw it, and I'll warrant he will have it visit him in his dreams—that old mother roasting, coiled in red hot steel springs and beside her brood of children! I tell you it was worse than pen can portray it."

The undertaker had problems getting the grotesquely contorted corpses into coffins. The funeral march to Harrison was haunting and somber. Then, several Black families fled the area. It was said that the "dreadful explosion" would "stand as a mark of happenings in the Mart region. 'This thing happening before,' and the other thing 'after dynamite night' will be fixed sayings with both white and black in that country."[51]

I COULDN'T FIND ANY evidence of the old Phillips place or anyone, Black or white, who knew anything about it.

As I wandered through the somewhat overgrown old Goshen African American Cemetery on the corner of a bend in FM 1860 in the old Harrison station area, looking for the graves of the atrocity's victims and that of Abe Phillips, I kept thinking about a metaphor in Booker T. Washington's Atlanta Exposition Speech of September 18, 1895, given two months after the retaliatory attack on the Phillips family. Washington probably didn't know about the Mart-area barbarity, but still.

> *A ship lost at sea for many days suddenly sighted a friendly vessel. From the mast of the unfortunate vessel was seen a signal: "Water, water; we die of thirst!" The answer from the friendly vessel at once came back: "Cast down your bucket where you are." A second time the signal, "Water, water; send us water!" ran up from the distressed vessel, and was answered: "Cast down your bucket where you are." And a third and fourth signal for water was answered: "Cast down your bucket where you are." The captain of the distressed vessel, at last heeding the injunction, cast down his bucket, and it came up full of fresh, sparkling water from the mouth of the Amazon River. To those of my race who depend on bettering their condition in a foreign land, or who underestimate the importance of cultivating friendly relations with the Southern white man, who is their next door neighbor, I would say: "Cast down your bucket where you are"—cast it down in making friends in every manly way of the people of all races by whom we are surrounded.*

Washington's comments were optimistic about progress, hopeful and practical—and probably useful to many. I wish more Texan members of the "friendly" vessel had bought in.

ALL THAT I DISCOVERED (and carefully avoided) in the Goshen Cemetery was snakes. Then I drove around and eventually spotted an elderly Black man in his driveway. I asked about the local Black graveyards and particularly the one in Old Harrison. He confirmed that it was the Goshen Cemetery and said he tended it when he had the time. I asked him if he'd ever heard of the explosion south of Mart, and he said he hadn't. I asked him if he had seen headstones for members of the Phillips family sharing the same date in 1895, and he said he wasn't aware of any.

A *Harper's Weekly* illustration from 1874. Southern racists utilized acts of terror, violence and intimidation to maintain white primacy. *Public domain.*

There were no "fixed sayings" regarding the act of terror that befell the Phillips family in 1895 and no sign of their remains. The local judge and law enforcement officers at the time believed that hostile neighbors had blown up the remaining members of the Phillips family to avenge the death of Phil Arnold, but no one was ever arrested, charged or prosecuted for the atrocity. West Phillips was apparently acquitted for shooting Phil Arnold, and Richard Bragg's wounds were not fatal. Bragg moved to Waco, but both he and Phillips reportedly spent the rest of their days dodging assassination attempts. In fact, an attack on Bragg's new residence was reported in the August 16, 1895 edition of the *Galveston Daily News.* Bragg survived once more, and the culprits behind the ambush were never apprehended.

The entrance to the African American Goshen Cemetery near Old Harrison Station in McLennan County. *Photo by author.*

Texas, again, is funny like that: long and tall on every myth and stray scrap of charming rustic lore, but short on remembering (much less owning up to) obvious malfeasance and monstrosity.

The Lone Star state is parched in more ways than one.

6

JOVITA IDAR'S SMALLPOX SCARS

"What on earth prompted you to take a hand in this?"
"I don't know. My…my code of morals, perhaps."
"Your code of morals. What code, if I may ask?"
"Comprehension."
—Albert Camus, *The Plague*

In 2020, the *New York Times* did a series of feature obituaries, titled "Overlooked." It was mostly devoted to women and "people whose deaths, beginning in 1851, went unreported" in the publication. It was an ambitious project, one that Texas itself, as a state and a society, would do well to replicate—especially since one of the most compelling figures examined in the series was Jovita Idar.[52]

The piece on Idar was particularly intriguing to me, because I had stumbled onto reports mentioning her family years before and, at first, didn't make the connection. When I started researching Idar for this book, I recalled the original link. I discovered that something had been missed or "overlooked" in all the new reporting and scholarship.

Idar was born in Laredo, Texas, on September 7, 1885. Her father, Nicasio Idar, was born in Port Isabel. Nicasio's father was a Portuguese sailor who was rarely around, and according to Idar's youngest brother, Aquilino,[53] his mother "sold" him to some cowboys for a year of work in Oklahoma when he was a teenager. Afterward, Nicasio got a job in the Nuevo Laredo railyards and worked as a yardmaster there for twenty years. Nicasio met Idar's mother, Jovita Vivero (of San Luis Potosi), in Rio Grande City. They married and had thirteen children,[54] of whom Idar was the second. Nicasio had done fairly well and settled in Laredo, where, in the mid-1890s, he founded *El Partido Independiente de Laredo* to help Mexicans and Mexican Americans there organize politically.

By 1896, Nicasio had been elected a justice of the peace. He and his wife's children were raised with the relative privilege of *la gente decente*[55] citizenry, and he placed a special emphasis on education and public service. According to Aquilino, he often discussed these matters with them.

A Lone Star legend, journalist and activist Jovita Idar defied the Texas Rangers and the Catholic Church and fought for the rights of Mexican Americans. *Public domain.*

> *Out in the yard, my father used to sit right there and all of us—seven brothers and two sisters, used to form a circle around him. And he would talk to us about Mexicans, about Mexican-Americans; how to fight for the Mexican people; what to do for the Mexican people. How to think. Don't let anybody tell you how to think, because you are a freethinker. You are standing on the face of the earth on your own two feet. So use your own brain to work your way up in any situation. He said, "You don't depend on anybody to tell you that you're going to Heaven, to paradise, or this and that. You're gonna stay here until you die."* [56]

Jovita Idar was able to attend the Laredo Seminary (later known as the Holding Institute),[57] founded just three years earlier by the Methodist Episcopal Church. From here in examinations of her life, most narratives—including the *New York Times* "Overlooked" account—jump to her father's activism and his work as the editor and publisher of *La Crónica*, a local Spanish-language newspaper. But there was more to Nicasio's progressive work. It included membership in Mexican Tejano social and fraternal orders in the Rio Grande Valley, including the Masonic-structured Gran Concilo de la Orden Caballeros de Honor, of which Nicasio was the Laredo lodge secretary. And *Crónica* articles reporting on the lodge parroted

Nicasio's views. A December 17, 1910 article titled "Excitativa Del Gran Concilio de La Orden Caballeros de Honor a La Raza Mexicana," is almost striking for its candor:

> *It is not possible…to attain respectability, trust, and protection within the American nation, if we ourselves do not have this with our co-nationals; if we believe that the Mexicans are unworthy of our association with them, of us joining their associations, we should not expect that the Americans would gladly receive us in theirs. If we do not have trust in the men of our own race how can we expect other races to have trust in us?*

As Gabriela González puts it in *Redeeming La Raza: Transborder Modernity, Race, Respectability, and Rights* (2018), the article "critiqued the divisions among méxicano-tejanos, particularly the selfish shortsightedness of the comfortable class for their lack of loyalty to the group and their lack of respect for Mexicans of modest means."

After Idar's graduation and attainment of a teaching certificate, she worked as a teacher in Los Ojuelos, a small community between Laredo and Hebbronville. But Idar was discouraged by the conditions and school facilities in the community,[58] and she reportedly resigned and decided to work with her father and two of her brothers, Clemente and Eduardo, at *La Crónica*. In *Crucible of Struggle: A History of Mexican Americans from Colonial Times to the Present Era* (2011), Zaragosa Vargas notes the ways "the Idar family sounded off in the pages of *La Crónica* against separatist and inferior housing and schools, the abysmal conditions faced by Tejano workers that took on the visage of peonage and the gross violations of Tejano civil rights." And this at a time when, as the "Overlooked" story describes it, "Laws of the Jim Crow era enforcing racial segregation also limited the rights of Mexican-Americans in South Texas (they are often referred to by scholars today as 'Juan Crow' laws).[59] Signs saying 'No Negroes, Mexicans or dogs allowed' were common in restaurants and stores. Law enforcement officers frequently intimidated or abused Mexican-American residents, and the schools they were sent to were underfunded and often inadequate. Speaking Spanish in public was discouraged."

Idar herself was particularly compelling. Often composing diatribes under pen names like Ave Negra (Spanish for "blackbird") and Astraea (the Greek goddess of justice), she tirelessly advocated for Mexican Americans and, particularly, women,[60] asserting that they should educate themselves and not acquiesce to lives of subservience to men or, for that matter, the

Jovita Idar and two of her brothers standing in the production offices of *La Crónica*, circa 1910. *Courtesy of the Archives for Research on Women and Gender, Special Collections and Archives, Georgia State University.*

patriarchal Catholic Church. For *La Crónica*, it verged on a crusade. The publication openly blamed religious fanaticism for Mexico's staggering illiteracy rate, noting that "eighty-three percent (of the Mexican Republic) are illiterates who vegetate like pariahs, unconscious of their existence and ignorant of their rights and duties as of a Republic that proclaims to figure in the vanguard of the most cultured and powerful nations on earth."

A controversial anonymous article in the February 2, 1910 edition of *La Crónica* warned of the patriarchal monopoly of the Catholic confessional:

> *The confessional scares me, and I advise mothers to teach their daughters to confess their guilts and faults not to God, or to confess them before the lattice of the confessional, to the ear of a man who has no right to listen to the conscience of youth, and who is susceptible to feel all of the human passions precisely because he is human and celibate. The mother loves her daughters with heartfelt, immense, pure and incomparable love, and she is the legitimate confessor of the family and the legitimate counselor of the home.*

Then, a week later, a *Crónica* piece titled "Vulgariza La Revista Catolica" clarified the publication's position: "We do not want the woman to stop believing in whatever God strikes her fancy….We only want to destroy the idols of the woman's heart and have her turn her face once again to her God so that she can adore him with more intelligence, freely."

By the time "Debejamos Trabajar" appeared in the December 7, 1911 edition of *La Crónica*, Idar had secularized the sentiment so that it appeared more palatable (if not more digestibly feminist): "Working women know their rights and proudly rise to face the struggle. The hour of their degradation has passed…they are no longer men's servants, but their equals, their partners." And she was known to take it even a step further, flatly proclaiming, "Educate a woman, and you educate a family."

"Jovita worked toward the creation of a better world where women and men of all backgrounds would be able to thrive and contribute to their communities," said González, an associate professor in the history department at the University of Texas at San Antonio, in a 2017 *San Antonio Express-News* interview. "She labored for social justice, for an end to racism and segregation, for women's rights and for the rights of children to have an education and therefore greater opportunities."

Idar and her family utilized *La Crónica* to support the creation of El Primer Congreso Mexicanista (the First Mexican Congress) to advocate for justice and equality for Hispanic people in Texas. The Congreso met for eleven days in September 1911. They recognized Mexican American achievements, celebrated their Mexican heritage, sponsored empowering speeches and staged festive community performances. Idar and other women were prominent participants in the event and subsequently formed the Liga Femenil Mexicanista (the League of Mexican Women), of which Idar was the first president.

In 1913, Idar crossed into Mexico and worked with La Cruza Blanca (a medical aid organization like the Red Cross) during the Battle of Nuevo Laredo in the Mexican Revolution.

La Crónica closed its doors after Nicasio's death in 1914, and Idar became a staffer for another Spanish-language newspaper in Laredo, *El Progreso*. When *El Progreso* published an editorial (by a Mexican revolutionary named Manuel García Vigil)[61] critical of the U.S. occupation of Veracruz later that year,[62] members of a local company of the Texas Rangers appeared outside the door of the offices of the publication, intent on shuttering it.[63] But they hadn't planned on encountering Jovita Idar. She promptly (and appropriately) berated them, reportedly issuing a succinct lecture on the First Amendment and freedom of the press. The Rangers retreated forthwith, returning the following morning (when Idar wasn't around) to destroy *El Progreso*'s offices and printing equipment and arrest the other employees.

IDAR'S STAND AGAINST THE Rangers was incredibly brave, considering their reputation for violence and bloodshed during encounters with Mexican and Tejano populations along the border at the time, and the history of her fearlessness and resolve is thankfully becoming more widely known. But a largely forgotten incident early in her life had a more profound effect on her and her family's social and political outlook and, perhaps, on the city of Laredo itself, as this incident shaped the family's views thenceforward. This incident was known as the Laredo Smallpox Riot. A brief account of the riot is available on the Texas State Historical Association *Handbook of Texas* online.

> *LAREDO SMALLPOX RIOT. A smallpox epidemic at Laredo that began in early October 1898 led to events that eventually climaxed in March 1899, when a violent showdown between Mexican Americans and Texas Rangers resulted in the immediate death of one man, the wounding of thirteen, and the arrest of twenty-one participants. On October 4, 1898, Laredo physicians began noticing a disease resembling chicken pox among*

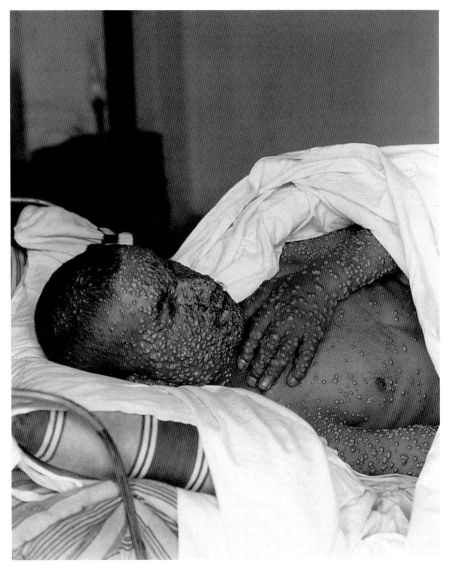

Young victim of smallpox, circa 1898. *Courtesy of Matson Photograph Collection, Library of Congress.*

the city's children. The first death directly attributed to smallpox, that of a Mexican child on October 29, prompted Mayor Louis J. Christen and local officials to start a committee to investigate reports of the illness. By the end of January 1899, more than 100 cases of smallpox had been reported in Laredo. Dr. Walter Fraser Blunt, State of Texas health officer warned that more systematic and thorough measures would have to be taken to control the epidemic. Dr. Blunt's instructions included house-to-house vaccination and fumigation, the burning of all questionable clothing and personal effects that could not be fumigated, and the establishment of a field hospital to disinfect patients. This field hospital was in effect a quarantined area, referred to as the "pesthouse." Most of the vaccination and fumigation efforts were directed at the poorer barrios of the city along Zacate Creek on the east side of town.

Conditions worsened to such an extent that on March 16, 1899, Blunt arrived from Austin to take charge of efforts to control the epidemic. A serious problem arose when a number of Laredo residents began to resist the vaccinations and fumigations. Blunt responded by requesting the services of the Texas Rangers to help medical teams carry out house-to-house vaccinations and fumigations. On Sunday, March 19, 1899, a small detachment of rangers arrived from Austin and joined in the efforts to get all residents immunized. The arrival of the rangers heightened the apprehension of some people being forced to submit to the radical health measures. Friction between Mexican Americans and Texas Rangers was long-standing in South Texas. Where the rangers met resistance, they broke down doors, removed occupants by force, and took all who were suspected of having smallpox to the pesthouse. A throng of angry protesters gathered and showered the rangers and health officials with both words and rocks. In the ensuing melee, Assistant Marshal Idar was hit on the side of the head by a stone, and one of the protesters, Pablo Aguilar, received a shotgun wound in the leg.

"Assistant Marshal Idar" was Jovita's father, Nicasio.

As educated members of *la gente decente*, Jovita Idar's family found themselves caught between historically abusive and overbearing American law enforcement agencies and medical officials (on one side), and the uneducated, "pariah"-like members of their fellow Tejano and "conational" community on the other.

The next day the Laredo Times reported that Deutz Brothers, a local hardware store, had "received a telephone order for 2,000 rounds of buckshot to be delivered to a certain house in the southeastern portion of the city, but instead of filling the order the authorities were notified and given the location where the delivery was to be made." Sheriff L.R. Ortiz quickly obtained a search warrant and took with him Capt. J.H. Rogers and his detachment of *Texas Rangers*. *The elite squad had been reinforced that morning with the arrival of more rangers on the train from Austin. Together they began a house-to-house search in the immediate area where the ammunition was supposed to have been delivered. At the home of Agapito Herrera, trouble began for Sheriff Ortiz and the rangers. Herrera, a one-time Laredo policeman, met the lawmen outside his home and took Ortiz aside to talk privately. As the discussion heated up, a youngster standing in the doorway shouted "ya!" and darted inside. Almost simultaneously, while the nervous rangers drew their guns, Herrera disappeared into the house and ran out the back door accompanied by several armed men. In the ensuing gunbattle, Captain Rogers was wounded in the shoulder by a bullet fired from Herrera's pistol. Herrera himself was shot in the chest by ranger gunfire. Ranger A.Y. Old ran up to the wounded Herrera and pumped two fatal shots point blank into his head. The dead man's sister, Refugia, was shot in the arm, and a friend, Santiago Grimaldo, was shot in the stomach.*

After evacuating Rogers, rangers returned to find an angry crowd of about 100, some of whom were armed, gathered around Herrera's lifeless body. After the hurling of more taunts, someone in the crowd fired a shot. The rangers promptly opened fire into the crowd, wounding eight, including one man mortally. As evening approached, the rangers retreated to Market Square. All through the night, sporadic gunfire could be heard in the same troubled neighborhood. Realizing that the situation could easily worsen, the rangers called on the cavalry unit stationed at Fort McIntosh for additional support in restoring order. On the morning of March 21, the Tenth United States Cavalry [comprising African Americans], *under the command of Capt. Charles G. Ayers, moved into the affected neighborhood to maintain the peace and assure that the work of controlling the smallpox epidemic continued unhampered. Rangers also patrolled the area, searching for and arresting anyone they thought involved in the riot. Liberal journalist Justo Cárdenas and twenty others were arrested. Few disturbances were noted in the days that followed. The army seemed to have taken control of the situation, and Mayor Christen pleaded with other areas of the state to send food and clothing to the victims of the epidemic. Throughout March many children continued to die of smallpox, but in April the number of deaths decreased dramatically. The situation had improved so much that by May 1, 1899, Blunt ordered the quarantine lifted.*

Today, one in five Texans is still not vaccinated for COVID, and certainly during the heights and leveling off of the COVID pandemic, our uneducated, ill-informed or ignorant, "pariah"-like neighbors (of all ethnicities) reacted in much the same way their counterparts did in Laredo in 1899. The difference, however, is that the undereducated and underprivileged members of the Tejano and Mexican community in Laredo at the turn of the nineteenth century had a legitimate excuse. They faced Juan Crow discrimination and underfunded education systems.

The Texans who verged on rioting and violence regarding the COVID vaccinations at the dawn of this millennium had complete access to informational opportunities and educational programs, and their obliviousness to public-health considerations and borderline spiteful intransigence is still inexplicable and stupefying.

Unlike many contemporary Anglo-Americans today, however, Jovita Idar's family seemed to bear Nicasio's attackers no ill will, and the patriarch, two of his sons and his daughter set out to help them via education and by providing an alternative, cogent voice in the Mexican American population's ongoing struggles for equality and justice in Texas. And they did so not for monetary reward, fame or political gain, but for the future of La Raza.[64]

IDAR MARRIED BARTOLO JUAREZ in 1917 and moved to San Antonio. Though childless, she helped raise the children of her sister Elvira, who passed away during childbirth. Idar established the Democratic Club in San Antonio and became a precinct judge for the party. She also created a free kindergarten and served as an interpreter for Spanish-speaking patients at a local hospital.

Idar struggled with tuberculosis for many years and succumbed to a pulmonary hemorrhage at the age of sixty on June 15, 1946.

7

SNOWBALL'S CHANCE IN HILLSBORO

White Texans specialized in burning Blacks alive.
—Walter L. Buenger,[65] *Southwestern Historical Quarterly*
(July 1999–April 2000)

I f you live in a place long enough, you begin to think you know it, or
that it defines you or becomes part of your DNA. And if you were born
there, its role in your identity is official. But that certainly wasn't how I
felt at the March 8, 2022 regular meeting of the Hill County Commissioners
Court in Central Texas, particularly when, after a pledge of allegiance to the
American flag, we were expected to pledge our allegiance to the Texas flag. I
didn't even know Texas had a pledge of allegiance, and I certainly was never
asked to perform one when I was in school. I didn't even know the words. I
just kept my right hand over my heart and mumbled through it.

It was off-putting, and I looked it up when I got home that evening.
A pledge of allegiance to the Texas flag didn't become official until two
conservative lawmakers co-sponsored a bill in 2003 requiring schoolchildren
to recite it along with the national pledge. This surprised me. I'd lived my
whole life in Texas and had no clue. So there I'd been, standing in the gallery
of the Hill County Commissioners Court, pretending to make the pledge
with three Black women and two young Black boys.

IT ALL STARTED IN early January 2022, when a sixty-eight-year-old Black
woman named Crady Johnson contacted me about a piece I'd written in
the *Fort Worth Weekly* three years earlier. "Dull in the Heart" was about

Left to right, Letha Young, Tonya Camel and Crady Johnson standing at the spot where Bragg Williams was burned at the stake in 1919. *Photo by author.*

Bragg Williams, an intellectually disabled Black man who was burned at the stake in Hillsboro, the Hill County seat, in 1919. My story had run close to the centennial of the incident, and Crady had just stumbled onto it. A lifelong resident of Fort Worth, Crady is Williams's niece. She wanted to know more about me and more about what I knew regarding Williams. She and her fifty-seven-year-old niece, Tonya Camel, also a resident of Fort Worth all her life, had heard their Uncle Bragg was lynched, but Crady's mother never talked about it much. My narrative shocked them. Crady invited me to meet with her family at a restaurant in the Mid-Cities, and I accepted her invitation.

By the time we got together, Crady and some of Williams's other relatives had done their homework. They were familiar with my *Slocum Massacre* and *Black Holocaust* books and knew I had worked with descendants of victims of the Slocum Massacre to attain the first state historical marker specifically acknowledging racial violence against African Americans in Texas. The meeting was somber but congenial. I shared what I knew, and they shared what they were aware of. I told them the "Dull in the Heart" piece was an expansion of an excerpt from *Black Holocaust*. We had a nice conversation about a dark subject, and we all learned some things. Then they popped the question. They wanted to know what I thought about trying to erect a historical marker acknowledging Williams's ghastly extralegal execution in Hillsboro.

"We needed to do something," Tonya said later, "because justice was never done, and Uncle Bragg never received due process, and nobody had to answer for it."

"We don't know what happened or whether Bragg was guilty or not," added Letha Young, Crady's eighty-one-year-old sister and a fan of TV Westerns. "The whole thing makes me think of *Hang 'Em High* with Clint Eastwood. He gets hung by some vigilantes for something he didn't do, but the sheriff comes along and cuts the hanging rope loose before Eastwood's character dies. Where was the sheriff or the police when Bragg was being burned alive on the courthouse square?"

I didn't sugarcoat things. I told Crady and the others that it would probably be a long, difficult grind. What I didn't tell them was that I wasn't sure if I was really up for another contentious, time-consuming marker effort. But in a way, I felt obliged. How could I turn my back on them or this history?

Why were so many white Texans bent on turning their backs on history?

IN THE EARLY AFTERNOON of December 2, 1918, Annie Wells and her son Curtis, who was almost five years old, were beaten to death at their home near Itasca. The husband and father, George Wells, had gone to Hillsboro, and the older Wells children were in school not far away. Annie and Curtis's attacker killed them and then carried their bodies into the Wells residence, setting it aflame presumably to destroy any evidence.

Neighbors and the Wells children, who were on their way home from school, saw smoke from the fire and retrieved the mother's and son's remains before they were badly burned.

The details of the case according to the January 18, 1919 edition of the *Hillsboro Mirror* are noted here.

> *Along the latter part of November, the Wells family was preparing to use their automobile, and a negro* [Bragg Williams] *working for them was starting the car, when he charged* [accused] *Mr. Well's* [sic] *little boy*

[Curtis] *with stopping the engine and the boy kicked him. The negro kicked him back and was discharged. On the second of December, while Mr. Wells was in Hillsboro the negro returned to the Wels [sic] home, and, according to the negro's story, Mrs. Wells asked him what he wanted and he told her work. She asked him why he kicked her son and began abusing him and struck him in the head with a broom she held in her hand. He grabbed the broom and she reached for a gun standing on the gallery. The negro beat her over the head, knocking her down and then hit her over the head twice more. Mrs. Wells [sic] little four-year-old son then started for the school house which was only a few hundred yards away, and the negro started after him and began hitting him over the head with the gun. Finding both mother and child dead, the negro drug both into the sitting room and piling cotton between them, set it on fire. He then went into the garage, which was built onto the house and to make sure of the burning of the building and thus destroying the evidence of his crime.*

The *Mirror* reported that, afterward, Williams went home, picked some cotton and was arrested by "Sheriff J.W. Martin" later while chopping wood. The *Mirror*'s report then stated that Martin and his wife (and someone named "Earl Pruitt and his wife") transported Williams to Hillsboro to turn him over to the local police.

The account of the transport reads more like a Sunday drive than the conveyance of a cold-blooded murderer to a jail. Reports, however, vary.

Described by the *Waco News-Tribune* as "tall and ungainly, and seemingly of low mentality," Bragg Williams was apparently taken into custody from the home he shared with his parents approximately three miles from the Wells residence; but before there had even been an official accusation made, a group of Hill County citizens attempted to lynch him, and Martin (with or without his wife and Earl Pruitt and his wife) had delivered the suspect to the home of a local attorney named W.C. Wear instead of directly to the county jail.

Martin solicited Wear's opinion as to whether or not Williams could have been the perpetrator of the crime and asked Wear to prepare a written statement for Williams to sign. Wear asked Williams to make a statement, and the suspect reportedly complied.

After hearing Williams out, Wear made remarks to Sheriff Martin that were disturbing. Based on his writings, he told Martin that "the people of Itasca community would come down before morning and kill the son of a bitch and they ought to kill him."

Falls County native and "alienist" W.L. Allison testified for the prosecution in Bragg Williams's trial. *Portal to Texas History.*

Wear insisted that "there was probably nobody in Texas more opposed to mob law than he, yet the facts as detailed by the defendant was [*sic*] so horrible that in this instance he felt an impulse himself to mete out speedy punishment."

Martin asked Wear what he should do with Williams, and the attorney was unequivocal. He said if Williams was placed in the Hill County jail, "he would be killed before morning" and others may be as well. Wear advised Martin to take Williams to Waco.

In early January 1919, Wear was asked by the Hill County District Court to defend Williams, but on January 11, Wear formally recused himself. The lawyer's recusal was appropriate and necessary, especially, perhaps, due to his expressed personal feelings of the incident as communicated to Martin, but Wear had also complicated the task of defending Williams by sharing the details of Williams's pre-Miranda, reportedly incriminating statement to others in Hill County. And this fact is recorded in Wear's official recusal request, the writings referenced above. He said the incident was so "unusual" that he referred "to the matter and made statements to various and sundry people as to what occurred."

On January 13, 1919, Texas governor William P. Hobby received an urgent communication requesting Texas Rangers to protect Williams. The message stated that "the prisoner was in imminent danger of being lynched," and the local sheriff (who was apparently named James Yancy McDaniel, not "J.W. Martin") had declared that not only would he not stop white citizens from lynching Williams, but he also opposed any attempt by Texas Rangers to protect the suspect. Governor Hobby sent Texas Rangers, and they transferred Williams from Waco to Dallas, where he remained until his trial date. On January 16, 1919, Williams was escorted back to Hillsboro by the Texas Rangers, and his trial began.

After Wear's recusal due to an arguably unconstitutionally procured confession and the irresponsible dissemination of the details of the reported confession, two highly regarded Hill County attorneys—Walter Collins and Albion M. Frazier—were appointed by District Court Judge H.B. Porter to defend Williams, and they did so under protest. They requested a change of venue for the case (in light of the certainty that the information that Wear shared had rapidly spread through the county), but it was denied. As the prosecution and defense seated a jury, Williams sat in the courtroom under the constant guard of six Texas Rangers.

Collins and Frazier entered a plea of "not guilty" for Williams by reason of insanity and, interestingly, protested the nomenclature of the case, *State of Texas vs. Bragg Williams, alias Snowball*. Williams apparently regularly wore faded khaki coveralls, and locals reportedly referred to him as "Snowball." In many settings, this alias arguably would have constituted a term of scorn or derision, perhaps especially to adult Black men of the period. The court's insistence on using it suggests a broad local familiarity with Williams, a possible "pet" nickname and, arguably, the kind of label a Black man of "low mentality" may not have minded. But for Collins and Frazier, it was at least a passive-aggressive form of denigration and had no reasonable bearing on the case.

In terms of the defendant's plea, not guilty by reason of insanity, Collins and Frazier specifically noted that "malice aforethought, which is absolutely essential to constitute murder, is where one with sedate, deliberate mind and formed design unlawfully kills another."

Collins and Frazier argued that Williams was intellectually disabled and that the evidence presented in the case would not rise above the threshold of reasonable doubt. They suggested that Williams's stunted intellectual capacity made him incapable of murdering someone with a "sedate, deliberate mind" and "pre-formed design," and they pointed out that—considering the defendant's intellectual disability—if Williams had, as accused, slain Mrs. Wells, it could have been due only to a perceived threat as interpreted from his limited cognitive perspective. This technically qualified the acts Williams was accused of as self-defense. This exact narrative was conveyed in the *Hillsboro Mirror*. The excerpts cited earlier from the January 18 edition of the *Mirror*, which were based on the confession that defendant Williams allegedly gave Wear (and that Wear admittedly spread), state that Mrs. Wells attacked Williams with a broom, which, in a cognitively impaired person's mind, may have constituted an imminent threat or have compelled a defensive response.

County Attorney Earl E. Carter and Assistant County Attorney H.P. Shead, however, were familiar with Williams's "low mentality" and anticipated the defense team's plea. The prosecution prepared a professional refutation. They brought in a Fort Worth alienist (the term for a psychiatrist

Bragg Williams's relatives standing at the door that was broken down to seize him in 1919. *Photo by author.*

or psychologist in those days) named W.L. Allison. A practitioner at the Arlington Sanitarium in Tarrant County, Allison was born in 1879 in Falls County, a hotbed of racial violence during Reconstruction and well into the 1890s. He undermined the defense team's insanity plea before the all-white, all-male jury.

Williams never testified in court, but a sizable portion of the community must have been aware of his statement to Wear, and he did apparently return to Hillsboro in the same khaki coveralls that he had left in—the coveralls that identified him as "Snowball." The prosecution subsequently produced two white female witnesses who said they saw a Black man in "yellow" coveralls heading in the direction of the Wells residence before the murder, and a young Black girl, Smithy McDuffy, who claimed she saw a Black man in "yellow" coveralls running from the direction of the residence after she had heard the screams of Annie Wells.

A white jailer named Jess Vanoy testified that Williams had blood on his coveralls and shoes (presumably after Williams was apprehended). Williams's brother Natural was then summoned, and he testified that Bragg had blood on his shoes the day he was captured, but he didn't mention anything about blood being on his coveralls. All of this, of course, begged important questions. If the *Hillsboro Mirror* account of the crime was even remotely accurate, why wouldn't Sheriff Martin, Mrs. Martin, attorney Wear and Earl Pruitt and/or Mrs. Pruitt have been subpoenaed to confirm reports of blood on Williams's person—especially if he was wearing khaki coveralls, which would have made any amount of blood obvious?

Also, the details of the murder weapons were contradictory. *The Mirror* reported that Williams dispatched Annie Wells and her son Curtis with the butt of a shotgun. The court files indicate the weapons used to murder Annie Wells were the butt of a shotgun and a sharp instrument. The sharp instrument was never discovered or produced.

On Friday, January 17, Williams was convicted of murder, and the Texas Rangers were abruptly and surprisingly instructed to depart. Williams—arguably because he did not fully grasp the implication or the gravity of the court's verdict or sentence—laughed. The defense team's argument that Williams was intellectually disabled is perhaps nowhere better illustrated than with this laugh. The year was 1919, and the white-owned, white-run and white-staffed newspapers at the time would have focused on Williams's laugh if it had been in any way malicious, ill-intended or otherwise contemptuous or defiant. But no such reporting exists.

On the morning of Monday, January 20, the court reconvened for sentencing, and Judge Porter condemned Williams to be hanged by the neck until dead on February 21.

What happened next was completely unexpected.

Collins and Frazier had defended Williams under protest, and his guilty verdict was not an unpopular result. Once it was handed down and the death sentence was imposed, however, the two attorneys deemed it unjust due to the defendant's limited intellectual capacity and promptly requested a retrial. And when their petition for a new trial was denied, they immediately filed a notice of appeal to the Texas Court of Criminal Appeals.

At approximately 11:45 a.m., a mob—upset by the appeal and no longer in the mood for due process—assembled at the Hill County Jail and demanded Williams be handed over. The jailers refused to give him up, so the mob battered the jail door down, stormed the facility and seized Williams from his cell. The mob then dragged him to a concrete post at the intersection of Elm and Covington Streets on the southwest corner of the courthouse square and bound him accordingly.

A cadre of enthusiastic vigilantes quickly collected hay and wood and piled them around Williams, dousing the combustibles in coal oil. A match was then applied, and the conflagration killed Williams in a matter of minutes. Though he put up no resistance, he was heard to exclaim, "Help me, Cap," three times before the flames consumed him. Williams's body was reportedly left in the embers of the fire for hours. A photographer recorded the atrocity, and one Hill County lawyer is said to have kept one of the images framed in his office for decades.

On January 21, Governor Hobby denounced the lynching and initiated steps to investigate it. The next day, he sent a message to the Texas legislature requesting a law that would put an end to mob violence and correct the assumption that members of white lynch mobs were not prosecutable. Hobby's request was echoed by the National Association for the Advancement of Colored People (NAACP), which sent a telegram to Hillsboro officials demanding punitive measures against participants in Williams's lynching.

On the same day, the *San Antonio Express* published a condemnation of the Hill County court's decision to dismiss the Texas Rangers after the conviction. "If ever there was a fatal error of official judgment—whoever was responsible therefore—it was in this case. If ever there was a warning of lynching attempts, it was in this case."

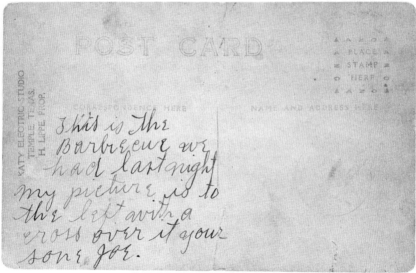

Postcard (front and back) commemorating the "barbecue" of a Black man named Will Stanley in Temple, Texas, on July 31, 1915. *Public domain.*

On January 23, Hobby instructed Attorney General Calvin M. Cureton, First Assistant Attorney General W.A. Keeling and E.A. Berry, assistant attorney general to the Court of Criminal Appeals, to initiate an investigation into the lynching of Bragg Williams.

A Hill County grand jury subsequently examined charges against members of the lynch mob but adjourned without returning bills of indictment. After the state investigation initiated by Keeling, Cureton and Berry filed a motion to cite twelve members of the lynch mob (Jud Rufus Beavers, Will Browning, Joe Ferguson, Cole Hammer, Earl Hobbs, Jim Hobbs, William Pinckney Hightower, E.L. Stroud, George Wells, William R. Wells, Poly Wilson and Wiley Wilson) for contempt of court in regard to the Court of Criminal Appeals motion, because the vigilantes had lynched Williams after his appeal had been filed and was technically pending.

The effort was a well-conceived attempt to prosecute members of the lynch mob in a higher court, especially as it was obvious that they would not face prosecution in Hill County. The motion was described as the first of its kind in Texas, but it, too, fell short. No action was taken on the motion in March or April, and the attempt quickly faded into obscurity.

WHEN I SPOKE TO Crady, Letha, Tonya (Letha's youngest daughter) and several other family members in late January 2022, they hadn't even been aware that Bragg Williams was intellectually disabled. Their family had fled Hill County after his horrific lynching, and no one talked about it a lot after. One story that survived was of Williams's mother walking several miles with one of his infant siblings on her hip to visit him at the Hill County Jail. On arrival, she learned that he'd been transferred to Dallas. The Hill County authorities hadn't even notified his family.

Crady, Tonya and Letha didn't procrastinate. They quickly decided to pursue a historical marker acknowledging the lynching and enlisted me to help write the marker application. When we first appeared at the Hill County Commissioners Court a little early on March 8, one of the commissioners asked us why we were there. When we told him why, he said we weren't on the docket and that we wouldn't be able to address the court. The court clerk we approached to verify this claim informed us that this was incorrect, so we seated ourselves in the courtroom and waited.

After the two pledges of allegiance and regular county court business was concluded, I addressed the commissioners court and explained our intentions. County Judge Justin Lewis and the commissioners present didn't seem completely amenable, but they weren't openly hostile, either. And, afterward, Judge Lewis came over and talked to Crady, Letha, Tonya and me and admitted that a cruel injustice had been committed in Hill County after the Bragg Williams trial and that he didn't think we would have any problems procuring a marker. I was skeptical, but Lewis seemed amicable and straight shooting, and we appreciated his speaking with us.

On April 5, I submitted the preliminary marker application (with Crady Johnson listed as the primary sponsor), and on April 18, the Hill County Marker chair, Jana Burch, let us know that the marker narrative was missing a context section, that there was no evidence that Williams was intellectually disabled and that the application needed to be better documented. It frustrated us, but we dug deeper, went to some lengths to substantiate claims of Williams's cognitive impairment and addressed the documentation issues. The marker application increased from ten to twenty-one pages, and we resubmitted it.

FOR A DISCUSSION REGARDING the context of the Hillsboro lynching of Bragg Williams, it is necessary to examine the history of lynching in the region and, perhaps specifically, burnings at the stake.

On July 22, 1910, Henry Gentry, an eighteen-year-old Black suspect accused of "peeping" at a white woman through a window in her home and killing a constable, was stripped naked, dragged around the Bell County courthouse square (by a horse at full gallop) and then burned at the stake on the courthouse grounds. On July 31, 1915, Will Stanley, a thirty-one-year-old Black suspect accused of murdering three white children in Temple, Texas, was shot and dragged through a fire repeatedly until the hellish flames silenced his cries and moans. And on Monday, May 9, 1916, Jessie Washington, another reportedly intellectually disabled eighteen-year-old African American man accused of bludgeoning a local white woman to death, signed his "X" to a confession he couldn't even read in Waco. Washington was arrested, indicted, tried and convicted, but before the presiding judge could even record the speedy guilty verdict, a large man in the rear of the McLennan County courtroom shouted, "Get the nigger," and a mob seized Washington. They burned him at the stake as the Waco mayor and chief of police looked on.

There were other disturbing incidents in the Hillsboro area. A Black suspect named Zeke Hadley was lynched on June 23, 1884, for the suspected rape of a white woman, and Hill County citizens attempted to lynch Isaac Bruce, a twenty-something Black man falsely accused of raping a white girl in 1892. Though the attempted lynching of Bruce was unsuccessful, some of the same men who tried to lynch him served on the all-white, all-male jury determining his fate. Bruce's defense team presented credible witnesses and mounted a strong defense, but the jury found Bruce guilty, and the presiding judge sentenced him to death. An all-white court of criminal appeals subsequently affirmed the conviction, but in mid-May 1893, Texas governor James S. Hogg commuted Bruce's death sentence to life in prison "to spare his life and await future developments." Hogg's instincts were correct. Bruce was later pardoned and released.

These incidents and numerous others all have some bearing on the general proclivity for the white citizenry in Central Texas to conduct or condone grotesque lynchings in that era, but the underpinnings of Hill County race history are even darker. For example, examine the page on the Hill County Rebellion in the historical association's *Handbook of Texas*.

> *HILL COUNTY REBELLION. During Reconstruction Governor E.J. Davis and the Radical Republican–dominated Twelfth Legislature of 1870 attempted to control crime in the state. In October 1870 Davis threatened Hill County with martial law for its tolerance of criminals. Conditions in the county seemed improved by late 1870, but in December a freedman and his wife were murdered in neighboring Bosque County, and State Police Lt. W.T. Pritchett moved into Hill County chasing suspects James J. Gathings, Jr., and Sollola Nicholson. Pritchett raised the ire of James J. Gathings, Sr., by seeking to arrest his son. The elder Gathings, Hill County's largest landowner, incited a mob that pushed county officials to arrest and detain the State Police troopers in Hillsboro in early January 1871. On January 11 Davis declared martial law in Hill County and dispatched Adjutant General James Davidson and the State Militia to rescue the jailed police.*

This "General Entry" citation contains mistakes and leaves out a lot of the story.

First, Hill County's "tolerance of criminals" especially favored acts of violence against persons of color. Second, the December double murder didn't befall "a freedman and his wife." It was Joe Willingham and the wife of Lewis Willingham, both longtime, peaceable residents of Meridian, Texas. Third, on June 18, 1870, a Black man named Thomas Tanner was murdered in Hill County, and six other African Americans—Tanner's neighbors—fled to McLennan County, declaring "that no protection was afforded to blacks" in Hill County and that they were afraid to stay there. And fourth, after whites burned down a Black school near Towash on October 21, 1871, Hill County could no longer hire or retain qualified instructors. During the same period, whitecaps (terrorist precursors to the Ku Klux Klan) actually ran a

The charred remains of Jessie Washington in Waco, Texas, on May 15, 1916. *Courtesy of the Library of Congress.*

Black man out of Hill County for engaging in a dispute with a white man. And it was not uncommon for whites in some Central Texas counties to try to expel all Blacks from county boundaries altogether. Hill County never officially went so far as that, but the lawlessness it permitted against its Black citizenry was as effective as doing so. As Barry Crouch and Donaly Brice state in *The Governor's Hounds: The Texas State Police, 1870–1873*, "Hill County blacks, although they composed but a fraction of the total population, found themselves on the receiving end of outrageous acts" of murder and terrorism—and the perpetrators of those acts were never held responsible or punished.

On January 25, 1919, the *Dallas Express* said that, with the lynching of Bragg Williams, Hillsboro could step "into the Limelight" of white primacy. Williams's burning was the first major racial incident in Texas in 1919, and it was the first lynching mentioned in the NAACP's historic fifteen-page pamphlet of February 1920, "An Appeal to the Conscience of the Civilized World."

ON APRIL 28, CRADY, Tonya, Letha and I resubmitted the application and then got back on the schedule to meet with the Hill County Commissioners Court for its permission to place the marker on the courthouse square (so our marker application could be forwarded to the state). In the interim between our appearances, a white woman named Katie Schatzlein reached out to me after reading *Black Holocaust* and shared a story. Schatzlein said that when the Hill County Courthouse burned on New Year's Day in 1993, she telephoned her mother to express what a shame it was, because she thought the Hill County Courthouse was one of the most beautiful buildings of its kind in Texas.

"Knowing nothing of the history of the Bragg Williams lynching," Schatzlein said, "I expressed sadness at the courthouse's loss."

Her mother's response was shocking. "That's when [my mother] said, 'Perhaps it's poetic justice or karma.'"

And then the mother broke down and shared the whole story. Schatzlein's mother told her that her grandfather had participated in the Bragg Williams lynching and drank himself to death at the age of fifty-one, perhaps because of his guilt. Schatzlein asked her mother why she never told her, and the mother said it was because of the guilt that she, herself, had always felt. The mother lamented the fact that she had never done anything about it, but she said she was telling Schatzlein then because perhaps she could do something.

When Crady, Letha, Tonya and I appeared in front of the Hill County Commissioners Court again on May 8, I still didn't know the pledge of allegiance to the Texas flag, but I planned to share Schatzlein's story. We all prepared ourselves to speak, but we never got the chance.

When Court Item No. "8. Discuss and/or approve for permission of Property Owner for Historical Marker placement" came up, there was no "discussion" at all. Judge Lewis immediately called for a vote, and the board approved the motion unanimously.

Crady, Letha, Tonya and I were surprised. Each of us, in our own way, had prepared to make compelling remarks before the decision was put to a vote.

"I had prayed the night before," Crady said. "I had prayed that the words that came out of my mouth would be Godly words, words of forgiveness, words of love and compassion. I had prayed that whatever I said would be a reflection of my God."

After the Hill County Commissioners Court's affirmative vote on the location of the marker, Tonya sensed that something larger was at play. "It was divine intervention."

Crady concurred later in a phone conversation. "Even in the midst of all the anger and bitterness and strife and hatred we see these days, God is working, and not just for Uncle Bragg's family but for the people of Hillsboro."

In another phone conversation, Tonya added: "I think they needed justice, too. And maybe closure. It was a spiritual, humbling experience."

WHEN I PARTICIPATED IN the historical marker application process regarding the Slocum Massacre in 2014, application announcements had been made in late December. So, on November 2, 2022, I sent an email to the Texas Historical Commission attempting to confirm that our marker application had been passed along and everything was in order. I received a disturbing email in response to my query two days later:

> *The application for the Bragg Williams Lynching was received, however the application was canceled on October 10, 2022 due to the marker fee not being paid. We encourage you to re-apply next spring when our application period opens from March 1–May 15.*

I was flabbergasted.

I immediately phoned Crady and asked her if she'd received news of the application and she informed me she had not. I told her to check her email, and I contacted the historical commission. They confirmed the email, and I told them we'd received no word and that the marker sponsor may have missed the email.

Crady called me back, letting me know that she had unwittingly received the email but missed it, because she only checked her emails on her phone. She forwarded it to me:

> *Congratulations! The THC Commissioners have reviewed your application and staff will now be proceeding to the inscription. The marker fee is now due, payable and received in our office by 5 pm CDT on Friday, September 16, 2022.*
> *—THC Marker staff*

I was shocked and wildly dismayed.

The Texas Historical Commission representative was sympathetic but didn't know what could be done.

Crady and I were both frustrated beyond words. The marker application process had been tedious and frustrating, and we didn't want to have to refile. The announcement of the marker application's approval—which should have been a joyous occasion—was now a nightmare.

At this point, I sent a barrage of emails to the Texas Historical Commission and the Hill County Historical Commission. I wondered if it didn't fall under the Hill County commission's purview to make sure marker applicants were informed of the marker application decisions and particularly if they had

Left to right: Crady Johnson, Letha Young, E.R. Bills and Tonya Camel standing near the courthouse lawn spot where Hill County representatives informed us on May 8, 2022, that the Bragg Williams Lynching historical marker could be placed. *Photo by author*.

been approved. The Hill County Historical Commission chair and the Hill County Marker chair both informed us that they never received the email communicating the Bragg Williams Lynching marker application approval. On November 7, I reached out to the THC personally, expressing my concerns. I concluded with the following:

> *I don't know what is going on or why the incredible news that the Bragg Williams Lynching historical marker was approved was missed, lost or ignored, and I am not presently or officially pointing any fingers or disparaging any parties—but the news of what should have been an absolute good has been transformed into a nightmare. And a recurrent nightmare, at that. All the work, all the effort, the repeated trips to Hillsboro for the relatives, etc. It's disturbing. I beseech the commission to let us pay for the marker at this late date—regardless of mistakes, shenanigans, whatever. It's like the relatives of Bragg Williams made it all the way to the finish line on this and didn't realize they broke the ribbon or weren't informed of where the medal ceremony was. We did the work. We won the race. ?!?!?!?*
> *Please let us bring this effort to fruition.*

On Monday, November 14, 2022, the Texas Historical Commission re-sent the marker payment request, and remuneration was made immediately. A receipt of the payment's processing was conveyed to us by email on November 15.

The Bragg Williams Lynching historical marker should be dedicated in 2024.

We'll see.

8

THE DISINHERITED

Maybe they ought to lock the people up in the bank vaults
and let the money do the living.
—Philip Atlee, *The Inheritors*

In 1940, a volcano erupted in Fort Worth.

Let me repeat that. In 1940, a volcano erupted in Fort Worth.

In late October of that year, the gentlefolk of Fort Worth began to register unpleasant rumblings. Faint at first, the tremors quickly grew more noticeable and less infrequent. Coffeepots in mansions rattled just a little, and there were barely perceptible trembles of picture frames in local society halls. But then the rumblings became a gossipy din. Soon, the stately offices and brownstone porticos of the prodigally privileged were on full alert. And by the time the November 10, 1940 edition of the *Fort Worth Star-Telegram*—featuring notes on the cataclysm—was retrieved by servants from the most luxurious lawns or by most of the rest of our forebears from modest lawns, everyone knew why.

Virulent rather than violent, the volcano was not an earthen aperture protruding dramatically from the prairie landscape. It was the explosive response that a book elicited from the River Crest Country Club set. Its eruption was more literary than lava-based, but it blew chunks of Cowtown society improprieties sky-high (for all to see) and was followed by a spew of vitriolic outrage by the masters of Fort Worth commerce.

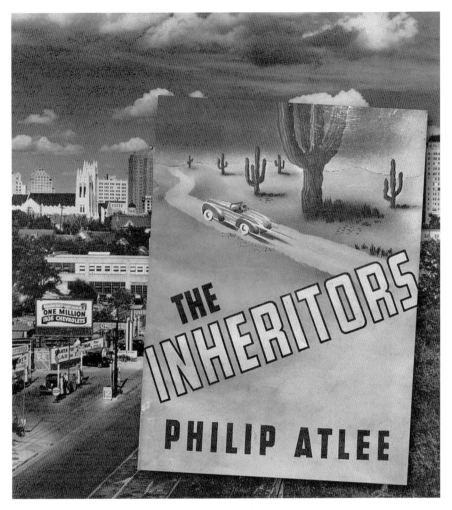

Cover of *The Inheritors* with 1940s Fort Worth backdrop. *Composition by author.*

Metaphorically speaking, however, their response would not resemble ancient Pompeii's. On the manuscript's release by the Dial Press on November 8, 1940, the offended parties immediately summoned and exercised the kind of absolute dominion that only the deepest pockets in American capitalism enjoy. And they wielded their control in a way that today's would-be and actual Lone Star political powerbrokers can only dream of.

The seismic, literary roman à clef behind the pre–World War II convulsion in Fort Worth was *The Inheritors*, and it was written by Fort Worth native James Young Phillips under the pseudonym Philip Atlee. Peruse, if you will, parts of the introduction and try to gauge the general indignance Cowtown "elites" must have experienced.

This is no golden legend. Instead, it is a bare, transcripted tale of youth. A guy named Mumford spilled a little blood on the story, and all of us helped the action along, but there was no great bravery involved. It all happened in Fort Worth, Texas, but that was only an accident of narration. The story could have been told anywhere in America, about any place that had a country club. Let no one think that the group herein described was atypical of youth. We were only a fringe, but there were a few of us everywhere. Many of our contemporaries, in the middle thirties of the twentieth century, led admirably sane lives and had a brisk Y.M.C.A. outlook. These are the ones who will undoubtedly save the country when the going gets toughest, but, as Cavin Jarvis said, they were damned uninteresting. I suppose the formation of character is a tedious thing...

The overlords of Fort Worth inhabited the quietest streets. Their large homes fringed the golf courses, and had three or four-car garages back of them. The interiors of these homes were lightened by pictures the owners did not understand or care to understand, and, in some cases, actually disliked. The wives of the owners were well tended and usually apprenticed to the intelligentsia. They were women who bought Shakespeare in handsomely bound volumes; they bought him and then had their maids dust him at regular intervals. The pages were usually uncut, but the owners were proud to have captured Shakespeare so that he could not get away. They trotted about, these women, to garden festivities and quick culture clubs, and they played bridge for rapaciously high stakes.

Their husbands did nothing but make money, but they could not be blamed for that. It was all they had been taught to do, and most of them were expert in the field. They were, for the most part, patient men who had been so strongly indoctrinated with the virus of the dollar aristocracy that they could not enjoy themselves fully even when they were financially able to do so. Therefore they were principally that sad sight, paunchy American business men floundering around, flailing ineptly at a white golf ball.

And set down in the heart of the town were the children of the country-club bludgeoners, the children who were being readied to catch the torch of Business. Not all of them were like us. We were well taught, but we were taught too much, and not of the right things. We drove fast cars and drank too much. The inference was given us, by well-bred curlings of the lip, that it was neither good nor desirable to be skilled in a trade. Instead, we were

113

taught to prize the professions, which insisted on the profit motif in every conscious act of life....

We were the inheritors in this last decade of the twentieth century.... We had no great respect for our elders, and we could smell, by some strange clairvoyance of despair, the neat destruction that was being built for us....

At this ripping, dream-destroying junction of responsibility and awakening, we needed meaning as individuals. We needed it badly....For lack of something to believe in, we came toward maturity as ill-met and unmannered pilgrims in a fog.

The first chapter begins with main character George Bellamy Jimble III (based on Phillips himself) waking with a hangover, and sophomoric episodes of masculine debauchery promptly ensue. Phillips's Jimble is a self-described "decadent Tom Sawyer," and his real-life friend Roy Lawrence Harris—depicted in the book as "Cavin Jarvis"—qualified "as a chromium-plated Huck Finn."

Phillips's Jimble and Harris's Jarvis are the two main characters of *The Inheritors*, and for the next two dozen chapters, they drink, chase girls, pursue a questionable easy-money grift for liquor money, express profoundly dim views of country club gaiety and undermine the entire Cowtown "dollar aristocracy" with unexpectedly powerful jabs and bull's-eye quips. After watching the attendees of an outdoor River Crest Country Club dinner, for example, Jimble silently observes that one very wealthy middle-aged couple nearby had little more to do then watch their fortune grow; they "were very careful people and ate every bite of their salads," Jarvis expands. "Can't be happy," he adds. "Too rich. Been rich too long, and they aren't people anymore. Just deadheading along until they grow cold." Then Jimble and Jarvis turn their attention to another wealthy couple. Jarvis delineates between the manicured twosomes. "Different. Entirely different. He's just passing through his money like a thirsty man passing through a green country. He's using it, making it buy him things. He knows there aint [*sic*] pockets in a shroud."

Roy Harris included *The Inheritors* as part of his Hollywood résumé. He would go on to appear in seventy-one feature films and over a dozen popular TV productions. *Courtesy of Jack Tillmany.*

"It could be," Jimble answers. "Maybe they ought to lock the people up in the bank vaults and let the money do the living."

Later, at the same gathering, Jimble and Jarvis's commentary becomes more incisive. When an orchestra begins to play, Jimble takes in the ostentatious display and flatly asks, "What's the good in it?" Jarvis stares at Jimble, his eyes smooth, "glazed by drinking" but unblinking. "The same song and the same singers," Jarvis says. "We're not people; we're just a set of attitudes walking around with logic-locked approaches to everything in life, and thirty phrases locked up in back of our teeth."

On another evening occasion as World War II approaches, Jimble's thoughts on a high balcony before inebriation once again holds sway are eerily prescient—for his generation and generations to come.

> *I tried to convince myself that I should not get drunk at the hotel, that I should be at home ruining my eyes over ponderous tomes concerning The Really Important Things in Life. I tried to think of one thing I could have learned in four colleges that would be an index to avoid fear of getting drunk or fear of being killed in a war started outside my ken and not touching me in any way....I tried to think of all my elders had taught me, and I tried to believe that some things were worth dying for, worth being gallant for, or even worth thinking of before sleep. But all my thoughts were flawed; they were all false rabbits and the hounds of belief would not run for them.*

Jimble and Jarvis and the rest still keep up the proper appearances. "The group of us, locked behind paneled doors and brocade curtains in an eyrie over the streets of Fort Worth, was conscious of knowing how to react conventionally under given situations, and of being a scrubbed and presentable segment of country club Christianity. We were all comforted by the unspoken realization, and so we talked earnestly, said nothing, and drank our drinks."

And in the end, the main characters—like Phillips's description of "Mumford," who "never lost his zest" and "was the nearest thing to a one-man revolution" Jimble was "ever privileged to witness"—all futilely tilt their lances at "capitalist windmills."

The book was a brilliant but scandalous marvel in its day, and those portrayed unflatteringly immediately forbade its presence and never forgot its author.

Harris (aka Cavin Jarvis) would show up in Hollywood and get on with Universal Studios shortly after *The Inheritors* was published, actually presenting copies of the volume as part of his résumé.[66] He would go on to act in nineteen films under his given name but, after serving in World War II, performed under the name Riley Hill. He appeared in more than seventy Hollywood films altogether and had a steady run on TV classics like *The Lone Ranger*, *Dick Tracy*, *The Gene Autry Show* and *The Range Rider* during the early 1950s. He played the apostle John in the 1952 series *The Living Bible* and spent the rest of the decade playing parts in *The Roy Rogers Show*, *The Cisco Kid*, *Adventures of Wild Bill Hickok*, *The Adventures of Kit Carson* and *Mackenzie's Raiders*.[67]

In terms of success and future prospects, *The Inheritors* would do the opposite for Phillips. The book faced the wrath of Cowtown's "dollar aristocracy" unbound. They bought up every copy they could find and no doubt dispatched threatening letters to the publisher in New York, where Phillips was then living. The book, the volcanic eruption and the volcano were snuffed out almost immediately, and Fort Worth went back to business as usual.

At the time, however, *The Inheritors* garnered no small amount of attention and some accolades outside of Texas. The December 1, 1940 edition of the *Baltimore Sun* called the book "unadorned and powerful and reminiscent of James Caine [author of *The Postman Always Rings Twice* (1936) and *Double Indemnity* (1936)] and the early Hemingway." The December 23, 1940 edition of the *New Republic* compared Phillips to another early twentieth-century literary icon.

> *Philip Atlee's lost generation of 1935 is so like Scott Fitzgerald's lost generation of 1918 that we can only conclude that if they drink enough, they all get lost. Atlee writes of the younger Country Club set around Fort Worth with a freshness and ease of a natural talent on the loose, and if he gets a touch sentimental trying to find cosmic meaning in their good time—after all, Fitzgerald got away with it, and there's nothing like trying.*
>
> *George Jimble III and a few other Dead End kids in white ties are the idle grandchildren of the old Texas oil pioneers. Their pranks and parties give the book the wholesome juvenile gaiety of a prom novel, even though the pranks verge on criminal and in less fortunate youths would undoubtedly send them up the river. Young Atlee's ebullient style, however, makes arson and rape and alcoholism seem like the sunniest bits of mischief, and no somber philosophizing on what's-the-world-coming-to can get him out of it. These folks live in a hangover haze that decent*

older citizens have striven to achieve, and frankly depict Fort Worth as a runner-up for the New Orleans festival crown. The scattering story has the vitality and conviction of scandal whispered in the cloakroom about the merrymakers you can glimpse in the ballroom beyond.

The author's statement that all the characters are no younger than eighteen and no older than twenty-five makes the romances a little less deathless; indeed the hardened old reader may become apprehensive lest one of the beautiful and willing young sirens end up permanently scarred by a Scout badge.[68]

Bett Anderson's review in the January 19, 1941 *Pittsburgh Press* was condemnatory and complimentary.

When Gertrude Stein addressed post-war youth with her now famous remark "You are all a lost generation," she did two things. She furnished flaming youth with one swell alibi, and she planted the seed for a perennial crop of for-tomorrow-we-die novels. The latest to join the chorus of the Stein Song is Philip Atlee with his book, "The Inheritors."

These "Inheritors" are a group of hard-drinking, slow-talking Texans who believe that their country clubs' verandas are their country's last frontiers. They were a part of the aspirin vanguard[69] *of the middle thirties.*

Specifically, this is a tale of George Jimble, Calvin [sic] Jarvis and Fred Bradley who thought that life was invented just to give them something to drink to. They were all selfish young men, and they were all blowing their own horn. Young Jimble stopped long enough to fall in love with Lucille Blenheim. A Fort Worthless lass belonging to the sisterhood of Lady Brett Ashley[70] *and the green-hated Iris March.*[71]

There is danger of taking a book like this too seriously. There is a greater danger in not taking it seriously enough. If you can wade through the unnecessary sophomoric smuttiness, there's some very fine writing to be found.

The preface is so good that I sincerely hope Mr. Atlee's next book will go on from there. If so, I'll promise to review it with an unprejudiced mind and forget all about George Jimble, the rich man's Studs Lonigan.[72]

Back in Fort Worth, however, *The Inheritors* was relegated to rash petulance and plebeian bluster. The dismantling of the book's import and legacy was practically already complete.

Before the book was released, the June 15, 1940 *Kirkus* review of the work was encouraging. "This is a book that will appeal to those who started on [F. Scott] Fitzgerald and followed through to [John] O'Hara [author of *Appointment in Samarra* and *Butterfield 8*], and who demand the best in that particular genre. It is even tougher than O'Hara; there's some of Caine's sadistic side; it is a full-blooded job, written in a virile, vital prose style which makes a terrific impact."

Philip Atlee's notorious roman à clef *The Inheritors* was compared to the works of F. Scott Fitzgerald (*above*), Ernest Hemingway, J.D. Salinger and others. *Public domain.*

The *Fort Worth Star-Telegram*'s November 10, 1940 post-publication review of *The Inheritors* concedes Phillips's obvious literary talent, but it concludes with a hardly coincidental—and probably obligatory—hatchet job.

> *As a first novel by a somewhat immature and confused young man, bewildered by his own task, The Inheritors is a flaming story of a group of over-age adolescents afflicted by their overstimulated instincts, their amorality and a rather stupid, cruel inheritance not of their own making… Any confidant of young Phillips knows he was deadly earnest, honest and even crusading when he wrote The Inheritors. Thereby, he fell innocently into the trap to "tell all." The novel suffers from an overextension of candor in several incidents that should have been saved for a privately-printed book of limited circulation. America, alas, is hardly mature enough for some of the scenes in The Inheritors, as artfully as they may have been described.*
>
> *From the standpoint of literary merit, The Inheritors reveals a young author with a poetic sense which follows him into the gutter, an insatiable curiosity about life which amounts to obsession, and a rare knack for apt phrases and meaningful words. The Inheritors may be a product of a poet who cannot quite turn realist without being nasty about it.*

Many contemporary Texas newspapers followed suit. The February 23, 1941 *Wichita Falls Times* review of *The Inheritors* panned it "because of the filth it descends to in places."

So, essentially, instead of noting this new, talented Fort Worth writer, Cowtown society dismissed him as a crank, disowned him and literally attempted (and, for the most part, succeeded) to erase him from the

Native Texan Katherine Anne Porter, journalist, essayist, short story writer, novelist, poet and political activist, was nominated for the Nobel Prize in literature five times. Courtesy of the Memphis *Commercial Appeal.*

annals of Fort Worth and Texas literary history. Meanwhile, inspired Cowtown chitchatters began creating and circulating textual keys that identified the real-life characters portrayed in *The Inheritors*' pages. Imagine if sales of the book had not been kneecapped. What status might it or its author have achieved in American letters?

The general public has a short memory and a limited attention span.

Fortunately, writers do not.

When George Sessions Perry—National Book Award–winning American novelist, World War II correspondent and one of the highest-paid magazine contributors of his era—put together *Roundup Time: A Collection of Southwestern Writers* in 1943, he included excerpts from the *The Inheritors* alongside those of John Steinbeck's *The Grapes of Wrath*, Oliver La Farge's *Laughing Boy* and works by J. Frank Dobie, Katherine Anne Porter, O. Henry, Conrad Richter and more.[73] This was no insignificant list of literary heavy hitters, and most appeared repeatedly in readers' digests and American lit classes for decades to come.

Some advocates suggested *The Inheritors* was an adult version of *The Catcher in the Rye* a decade before J.D. Salinger's adolescent classic written for adults, but *The Inheritors* was edgier and contained more heart and more honesty. A chapter near the end boldly and poignantly chronicles Jimble's trip with a young society woman to San Antonio for an abortion. It was scandalous in its day—it would probably get them both sued or arrested today.

In 1981, A.C. Greene, a widely respected Texas journalist, fiction writer, historian and book critic, published *The Fifty Best Texas Books*.[74] The list included the usual suspects, including *Coronado's Children* by J. Frank Dobie, *Blessed McGill* by Bud Shrake, *Pale Horse, Pale Rider* by Katherine Anne Porter, *13 Days to Glory: The Siege of the Alamo* by Lon Tinkle, *Hold Autumn in Your Hand* by George Sessions Perry, *Hound Dog Man* by *Old Yeller* author Fred Gipson and an unknown, lost classic that hardly anyone had ever heard of: *The Inheritors* by Philip Atlee. And Greene's remarks are worth sharing.

This isn't Cowtown. This is the young social set—carousing, driving big cars too fast, going from party to country club to any kind of devilment and eventual crack-ups—physical and mental. It's an overindulged generation.…The story is well done, and it was told thirty or forty years before its time. Few Texas books have been able to repeat the harsh dismay, the inspired brutality, of The Inheritors.

In *The New Frontier: A Contemporary History of Fort Worth and Tarrant County* (2006), Ty Cashion writes that *The Inheritors* "rocked Fort Worth society a generation before Grace Metalious' *Peyton Place* would cause the blue blood of New Englanders to run cold.…The wagging tongues of gossipers guessed at the thinly veiled identities of the characters, while the real-life subjects recoiled in indignation. At the library, so many books disappeared from the shelves the sole remaining copy was kept under lock and key, its readers assigned a place near the eyes of watchful staff members."

In 2011, Texas author Bill Crider brought the book up again, after grabbing *The Naked Year*, a renamed re-release of *The Inheritors* published in 1954. Crider called it "excellent writing" and "sort of a hardboiled Gatsby, set in Fort Worth." Except Fitzgerald's *Great Gatsby* buys into America's "dollar aristocracy" completely, while Jimble and Jarvis express open contempt for it.

In 2019, one day after his death, the *Big Bend Sentinel* published much-beloved Texas historian and raconteur Lonn Taylor's investigation into *The Inheritors* under the title "A Stealth Author from Fort Worth Is Revealed" in his theretofore syndicated column, Rambling Boy. Taylor said his story was "two years in the making," and it took him so long to finish it because he couldn't find anyone who actually knew James Atlee Phillips.

A 1961 graduate of Texas Christian University and actually a former student of the TCU instructor *The Inheritors* was dedicated to (Lorraine Sherley, namesake of the Lorraine Sherley Professor of American Literature at TCU endowment), Lonn Taylor was a former historian and director of public programs for the Smithsonian's National Museum of American History. Here in Texas, he helped curate exhibits for San Antonio's HemisFair in 1968 and, in 1970, became the director of the University of Texas's Winedale Historical Complex. After that, he served as a curator for the Dallas

The Grapes of Wrath earned John Steinbeck the National Book Award and a Pulitzer Prize for fiction and prominently figured into his Nobel Prize in literature in 1962. Wikipedia Commons.

Historical Society. In 1983, he also served as the guest curator of an exhibit celebrating the American cowboy for the Library of Congress. Taylor was no lightweight—and even he couldn't dig up much on Atlee.

But hardly could anyone else. As Taylor notes in his piece, "Copies of *The Inheritors* are as scarce as hen's teeth."

One of the only known copies around was tucked away in the Fort Worth Central Library's special collections. And, inside it, someone at some point wrote "Phillips, James Young" under the publisher-printed "Philip Atlee" on the volume's frontispiece. If you look up the author of *The Inheritors* on Wikipedia, his name is listed as James Atlee Phillips. As Taylor himself noted, Phillips was a "stealth author." This was a vast understatement.

JAMES YOUNG PHILLIPS—AKA JAMES Atlee Phillips, aka Philip Atlee—was born on January 8, 1915, in Fort Worth. His father, Edwin Phillips, was a lawyer for members of the River Crest Country Club's big oil families and made a handsome living. The Phillipses had a big house right off one of the greens of the River Crest Country Club golf course. Edwin was a member of the law firm of Phillips, Trammell, Chizum and Price; a director of the Farmers and Mechanics National Bank (before its merger with the Fort Worth National Bank); and served as the president of the prestigious Fort Worth Club. But in the late summer of 1928, he grew ill and, on September 5, succumbed to pneumonia.

Edwin's affairs were in order, and his wife, Mary Louise Phillips, and their children—Edwin Jr., James, Olcott and David—seemed at first to be fairly well provided for. But a little over a year later, the 1929 stock market crash wiped out the family's savings. James's youngest brother, David, would later comment on the drastic turnabout.

> *My father died when I was five, leaving my mother, three older brothers, and a portfolio of oil stocks which turned to ashes in the market crash of 1929. We were the poorest rich people in Fort Worth. A founder of a local country club, my father left us a life membership and the deed to a house on the fourth green.*[75]

Mary sold what she could from their big house and went to work for the Fort Worth Independent School District (FWISD). She and her sons were suddenly destitute in a mansion in one of the wealthiest neighborhoods in the nation.

If you recognize Mary Louise Phillips's name, it's probably because there's a FWISD elementary school named after her south of I-30 on the West Side. She worked hard and distinguished herself, and she did the best she could for her boys. In early 2022, Atlee Marie Phillips, forty-one—James Young Phillips's grandniece—told me that in everything she heard about her granduncle, her granddad and their brothers, she always sensed that they were profoundly affected by their sudden poverty in a neighborhood of such incredible wealth.

"It was really hard on them," Atlee said. "They tried to keep up appearances, and it was extremely difficult. And then Jim writes this blistering commentary about all of these people."

In a letter to his mother, who was a distant relative of Major Clement R. Attlee, lord privy seal and unofficial deputy prime minister of England[76] at the time (and Winston Churchill's chief adversary), Phillips shared his thoughts on *The Inheritors* (which he originally thought of calling *Threadbare Galahad*).

> *The characters are principally composite, but some situations are grounded on fact. I shall, in all possibility, create a tidy little corps of antagonists and it may even be that you will not like what I have done. But remember that I write no line, salacious, embittered or pornographic, that I didn't write truly.*

Mrs. Phillips, vacillating between pride in her son's writing and sympathy for those his sizzling prose offended and others who might criticize or even attempt to ban it, wired him this message: "Everyone will be shocked and no wonder. But Philip Atlee has written the truth about the thank god–small segment of youth which he knew. He writes with a wallop and is going to be a writer."

Or at least that was her son's plan, and the reviews almost everywhere except home seemed to reinforce his intentions. But the influence of the "dollar aristocracy" he crossed had scope and reach and doused his early aspirations before he got very far.

Then World War II intervened.

Phillips joined up, and many reports suggest he advanced quickly, first training pilots at Hicks Airfield north of Fort Worth, then serving in Burma and other spots in Southeast Asia. Then he joined the Marine Corps and spent the last two years of World War II working as the associate editor of *The Leatherneck*, the corps' official magazine. While editing *The Leatherneck*,

James Young Phillips (aka Philip Atlee, aka James Atlee Phillips), the greatest Texas writer that most Texans have never heard of. *Courtesy of* Fort Worth Star-Telegram.

he was also getting fiction published in magazines like *Collier's*, *Argosy* and *Blue Book*. After the war, Phillips moved to San Miguel de Allende in Mexico and was able to live there comfortably selling a couple of stories a year. When he and his first wife, former model Joyce Clayton—whom he married in 1940—divorced in 1949, Phillips returned to Burma. He worked for Amphibian Airways during the Burmese civil war and also had a stint at Cathay Pacific Airlines. Many assume Phillips was an intelligence operative during this period (if not before), but this claim has never been substantiated. His brother David, however, would become the head of CIA's Western Hemisphere Division, and many conspiracy theorists believe David was connected to the JFK assassination.

In 1952, Phillips relocated to the Canary Islands. In 1954, he ran into fellow Cowtown native John Graves, author of the Lone Star classic *Goodbye to a River* (1959), while residing on the main island of Tenerife. Later, in his book *Myself and Strangers* (2004), Graves writes that Phillips's frustration with the reception of *The Inheritors* had hardly waned. Phillips reportedly told Graves that he'd love "to buy a petty little atom bomb and at cocktail hour one afternoon he'd drop it down the chimney of the men's bar at River Crest Country Club."

Phillips would go on to dabble in Hollywood, helping to salvage the screenplay for John Wayne's 1952 film *Big Jim McLain* (which Phillips later called simplistic "anti-communist baloney") and the 1958 film noir *Thunder Road*, starring Robert Mitchum. Phillips also wrote for projects involving Jane Russell, John Forsythe and a young Stanley Kubrick. In 1963, he began writing the Joe Gall "Contract" series, the first book of which was *The Green Wound* (later changed to *The Green Wound Contract*) but also under the pen name Philip Atlee. The series would include twenty-two novels and win him an Edgar Award from the Mystery Writers of America in 1970. But perhaps the most important line in the entire series was the first line in the second chapter of *The Green Wound*: "The story of my life is: 'He rambled till they had to cut him down.'"

In 1984, the reclusive Phillips sat for an interview with Francis M. Nevins, an author of six mystery novels and, until recently, a professor at the St. Louis University School of Law. Nevins published the interview in his 2010 book *Cornucopia of Crime: Memories and Summations*. Phillips didn't say much about *The Inheritors*, but his fierce contrarian intelligence was on full display. The most telling exchange in the interview was initiated by Nevins, who told Phillips that what he liked most about his spy novel writing was the intriguing sense of moral and ethical schizophrenia—that unlike Ian Fleming's James Bond books, Joe Gall wasn't always shilling for the "good" guys. Phillips's response reminds us of everything we should admire in him.

> *That's because there was bifurcation in my own temperament. As a writer, I know that if you don't have the bullshit to keep it moving from page to page, you're going to lose readers. At the same time, I wasn't willing to admit to being such an absolute dunce that I didn't know it was bullshit in the first place....Gall knew what he had to do but he knew that it was a lot of bullshit, too, and that he was on the wrong side.*

Phillips eventually settled in Corpus Christi, where he died on June 2, 1991. His *New York Times* obituary referred to him as Philip Atlee, and most of the rest of the obits called him James Phillips or James Atlee Phillips. They all ignored Phillips's middle name, and this is unfortunate in its own right. His middle name, Young, comes from his maternal grandparents. His grandmother Mrs. G.A. Young, known to friends and relatives as "Mother Young," was active in the women's suffrage movement and organized women in Houston during one of the first elections in which women were allowed to vote.

THE FIRST MENTION OF *The Inheritors* I encountered occurred a little over a decade ago. I don't remember the exact circumstances, but I took note of it. Then I got busy with other things. When I did finally double back, I—like Lonn Taylor—couldn't find a copy. I just found a Judy Alter and James Ward Lee chapter on it in their 2002 book *Literary Fort Worth*, but the entire excerpt was basically just Phillips's take-no-prisoners introduction to *The Inheritors*—a passage of which I shared earlier in this chapter. Eventually, I became aware of the copy available at the Fort Worth Central Library and made three trips there to begin reading it. Then, again I got busy with other projects. But *The Inheritors* struck a chord that never stopped reverberating.

How could so few of us know about this book?

Class and wealth have always been a big thing in Fort Worth. My father, for example, grew up dirt poor on the south side of town, and he was not

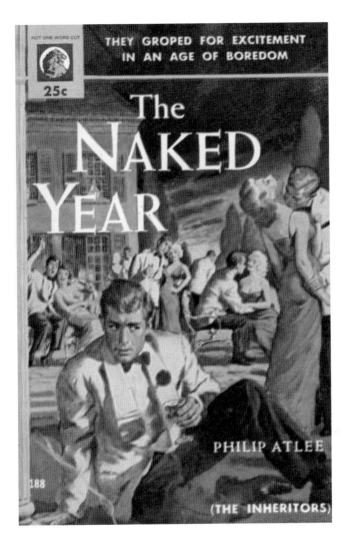

After being made to disappear for scandalizing the "dollar aristocracy" in Fort Worth in 1940, *The Inheritors* was re-released as *The Naked Year* in 1954. *Public domain.*

terribly welcome when he attended R.H. Paschal High School in the mid-1950s, when it was an institution for well-to-do and/or rich white kids. He and other students from low-income households were reminded of this fact often.

In the late summer of 1976, a plotline fit for a sequel to *The Inheritors* played out in what recently became a new Stonegate real estate development just east of Hulen Street, south of I-30. An intruder entered the former Stonegate mansion of oil tycoon Cullen Davis, one of the inheritors of the estate of Hugh Roy Cullen, patriarch of one of biggest oil fortunes in American history. Davis's former mansion (demolished in late 2021) was at the time inhabited by his second ex-wife, Priscilla Childers Davis, and the intruder killed her twelve-year-old daughter, Andrea Childers, and Priscilla's former TCU basketball star boyfriend, Stan Farr, and shot Priscilla herself. Priscilla staggered from the house while being pursued by the killer just as family friends Beverly Bass and Gus Gavrel Jr. drove up the mansion driveway. The killer shot Gavrel, paralyzing him for life, after Bass identified Cullen Davis as the pursuer and called him by his name. Priscilla identified Cullen to police, saying he had shot her and Farr, disguised only by a wig. Police arrested Cullen Davis that night at the house he shared with Karen Master, who would later become his third wife.

Davis, whose wealth was estimated at $100 million back then, was tried for the murder of Andrea but, even with two eyewitnesses, found not guilty. The prosecutor, Tim Curry, was blunt. He said the prosecution was "out-bought and out-thought." The trial of O.J. Simpson—who was not an inheritor—two decades later was a carnival sideshow compared to the Cullen Davis trial, because, at that time, Davis was considered to be the wealthiest American man ever to have stood trial for murder in the United States.

In 1985, R.L. Paschal High—by then a little less affluent, a little less well-to-do and a lot less white but still attended by children of the "dollar aristocracy"—produced the "Legion of Doom," a group of prominent, A-list, academic, athletic and inheritor-like white boys bent on enforcing their privilege and ridding their school of unwanted elements. They vandalized lockers and threatened classmates with guns. They built a homemade bazooka and a gasoline bomb. They denigrated poor kids and homosexuals, pipe-bombed a classmate's car and left a gutted cat splayed across another's steering wheel. But after they were finally caught and charged, they got a slap on the wrist. And many of the families who were part of the local "dollar aristocracy" openly sympathized with these young men who—let's be honest—ultimately committed acts of domestic terrorism.

A COPY OF *THE Inheritors* popped up on eBay in 2021, and I gladly overpaid for it. It wasn't in great condition, but it was worth every penny. I read it immediately, and I was amazed, dumbstruck and immediately otherwise busy again. But the antics of Texas state representative Matt Krause—who was campaigning for Tarrant County district attorney—made me pick *The Inheritors* back up and reread it.[77]

Late in 2021, Krause forwarded a now infamous letter to a Texas Education Agency official inquiring into 849 books in school libraries throughout the Lone Star State. The titles he focused on addressed topics including race and racism, sex and sexuality, abortion and reproductive rights and LGBTQ rights. In the letter, Krause wanted to know how much was spent on these books, which allegedly include material "that might make students feel discomfort, guilt, anguish, or any other form of psychological distress because of their race or sex."

In terms of Republican politics, it was typical but effective. GOP leaders are peerlessly adept at making political footballs out of anyone who isn't white, male and straight, but if you've lived in Fort Worth for a while and know about the "volcanic" eruption here in 1940, Krause looked more like a clumsy, bantamweight amateur than the true heavyweights of old. Back in the day, if the big boys had a problem with a book, they didn't wait for a local politician to do something about it. The big boys took care of it themselves. And they didn't bother with political theatrics or publicity-grabbing threats or bans.

They simply made the offending text disappear.

THERE IS NO QUESTION that the "dollar aristocracy" has done some good in Fort Worth (and Texas). And there's no way Cowtown would be home to first-class, internationally renowned art museums, a world-class zoo, the Van Cliburn competition, Bass Performance Hall, Amon G. Carter Stadium, Dickies Arena and more without our super-privileged overlords. But not everything they've done has been good, any more than everything they achieved was earned, much less good or right.

On July 1, 1862, the U.S. Congress enacted a "duty or tax" with respect to certain "legacies or distributive shares arising from personal property" being passed down, either by will or intestacy, from deceased persons to their descendants or heirs. The modern American estate tax was enacted under Section 201 of the Revenue Act of 1916. Section 201 used the term *estate tax*, but by the 1940s—just after *The Inheritors* was published—opponents of the estate tax began calling it a "death tax." In the 1990s, crafty Republican Newt Gingrich made hay out of this shrewd neologism, and now *inheritance tax* and *estate tax* are practically dirty words, and the fortunes passed down to the inheritor class aren't really taxed at all. Today, inheritors aren't just wealthy or politically connected. Like George W. Bush and Donald J. Trump, they often go on to run their state or the entire country. Or like Paris Hilton (an heiress of a vast Texan hotelier fortune) or the Kardashian ladies (whose lawyer father or stepfather was one of O.J.'s lawyers), they can have their own TV shows or clothing lines and make millions or billions on top of what they have already inherited.

That line from the November 10, 1940 *Star-Telegram* lambasting *The Inheritors* really sticks out now: "America, alas, is hardly mature enough for some of the scenes in *The Inheritors*, as artfully as they may have been described."

Sadly, it seems just as true now as it was then.

We were all cheated and disinherited by the Cowtown dollar aristocracy's sabotage and expurgation of *The Inheritors* and the potential literary legacy of James Young Phillips. And the citizens of Fort Worth and Texas remain the worse for it.

9

OPERATION UNRESPONSIVE

War is hell under any circumstances. But in the case of Americans serving these days in the Middle East, it's worse than that—it's a planned, coordinated societal psychosis.
If you plop a normal, all-American boy or girl down in a psychotic situation for months and years at a time, tour after extended tour, psychosis or extreme disturbance is not an abnormal response. And it can lead to suicide. Especially when the nation that sent these men and women into harm's way still hasn't honestly justified why this madness was necessary.
—E.R. Bills, "Johnny Got His Pills," *Fort Worth Weekly,* October 27, 2010

On Monday, March 13, 2023, a twenty-year-old Latina soldier from Long Beach, California, was found unresponsive at Fort Hood in Killeen, Texas. Her name was Ana Basaldua Ruiz, and she had previously complained about being sexually harassed at the base and admitted she no longer felt "comfortable" there.[78]

Private Basaldua Ruiz died under questionable circumstances. But she wasn't the first, and she won't be the last.

Award-winning investigative journalist May Jeong discussed the culture of Fort Hood in the July/August 2021 edition of *Vanity Fair.* "At first blush, such violence at a base that calls itself the 'Great Place' may seem extraordinary, inexplicable even. But then certain details start illuminating the mystery: that one out of every three women soldiers have experienced sexual harassment, according to a recent survey. That gun safety is a distant concern in a community where the Second Amendment tops the Maslow charts. That psychological trauma among veterans vastly exceeds physical wounds. That most soldiers enlist when they are still teenagers, their yet-unformed minds taught to kill. That American imperialism is imploding, and the blast force radiates inward."

More than a decade before Jeong explored the subject, I touched on an aspect of it in "Johnny Got His Pills" in the October 27, 2010 edition of *Fort Worth Weekly*. The title was a riff on Dalton Trumbo's unforgettable 1971 antiwar film.[79] I discussed the implications of the 2009 suicide of U.S. Army sergeant Douglas Hale Jr. After a stay in a Denton psychiatric hospital following his second (fifteen-month) combat tour in Iraq, he bought a gun in a pawn shop and shot himself in a restaurant bathroom. His final text read, "I love you mom im so sorry I hope u and family and god can forgive me."

In my editorial, I questioned the things that the U.S. military was doing to militate the toll of warfare and, specifically, the prescription of stupefacient (anesthetic, deadening, consciousness-dulling) substances to soldiers to help them navigate that "terrain." One of Katie Couric's producers subsequently emailed me, looking for more information on the subject.[80] It was exciting to see my work get that kind of attention. But the subject matter was terribly bleak.

I was writing pieces like that at the time because I thought they might contribute to a broader conversation. Attention from Couric's people was encouraging, but I don't know if they ever did anything on Sergeant Hale. And since then, things have changed. Stupefacient substances (including many formerly illegal ones that are now legal in some states) are in, and Fort Hood—in terms of nomenclature, anyway—is out.

Originally named after reckless Confederate general John Bell Hood (commander of the Texas brigade during the Civil War), Fort Hood is now Fort Cavazos—honoring the first Hispanic four-star general in Texas, General Richard Cavazos.[81] Military officials had until January 1, 2024, to finalize the change, and they did so on May 9, 2023.

Fort Cavazos is America's largest active-duty armored military installation, housing approximately forty thousand soldiers. Troops from Fort Hood and elsewhere have manned military operations in over eighty-three countries[82] since 9/11, including Operation Iraqi Freedom (March 19, 2003–August 31, 2010), Operation New Dawn (September 1, 2010–December 31, 2011), Operation Enduring Freedom (October 7, 2001–December 31, 2014), Operation Inherent Resolve (August 2014–present) and Operation Freedom's Sentinel (December 31, 2014–present). And according to the U.S. Department of Defense Casualty Status report dated February 21, 2023, in the course of these "operations," reported hostile and nonhostile U.S. military and U.S. Department of Defense civilian casualties have totaled 7,026.

The number of suicides among U.S. service members and veterans over the same period is a staggering 30,177. That's roughly 1,371 suicides a year, 115 a month and almost 4 a day.

That means that Sergeant Hale was hardly an anomaly.

That means the U.S. military had been conducting an unofficial operation as it simultaneously conducted Operations Iraqi Freedom, New Dawn, Enduring Freedom, Inherent Resolve, Freedom's Sentinel, etc. For now, let us dub it "Operation Unresponsive," because "unresponsive" is the standard cliché

In his farewell address, President Dwight D. Eisenhower warned, "In the councils of government, we must guard against the acquisition of unwarranted influence, whether sought or unsought, by the military-industrial complex." *Public domain.*

used to explain the condition of the victims when they are found intact in and around Fort Cavazos. And the command apparatus is consistently unresponsive to this issue, consistently unresponsive to the families of the victims and continually unresponsive or less than forthcoming to the press. And not just regarding the suicides or suspicious deaths, but also reports of sexual harassment, sexual assault (heterosexual and homosexual) and murder.

But what's a daily, weekly, monthly regime of murder, suicide and sexual harassment when a military base like Fort Cavazos, located on 218,823 acres in the Killeen area, contributes $28.8 billion to the Texas economy? Especially when that economy is largely based on fossil fuels and the U.S. military, again, is the biggest fossil fuel consumer on the planet. Is it a coincidence that we don't seem to go to war in many places where there isn't oil these days?

It's almost like Big Oil has its own military.

IT USED TO BE we sent American troops off to fight real wars against real enemies, not perform weapons testing, buttress the budget for the military-industrial complex (which President Eisenhower, a native Texan, tried to warn us about) or run errands for Big Oil. Today, however, our soldiers mostly only get to make or watch innocent brown people suffer overseas to make sure our Black Gold supply chain remains intact. We know it, and our victims know it. There's no honor in it, nor any real appreciation from the corporate entities it benefits the most. It's a charade we're all a part of but, as civilians, can accept and assume passive roles in. Stupefacient substances help with that. But our soldiers shoulder the active load—and it is a horrendous load. And this load has made places like Fort Cavazos more dangerous for U.S. soldiers than their actual deployments.

Ten years after my "Johnny Got His Pills" piece, Fort Cavazos was arguably growing more and more fubar[83] every other month. Twenty-year-old Specialist Shelby Tyler Jones died at a convenience store in south Killeen on March 1, 2020, after being shot at a local club. Some of his buddies reportedly tried to rush the native of Jena, Louisiana, to a hospital but had to stop at a store to render aid. Three months later, the case was "exceptionally" cleared and no one was prosecuted in Jones's death.[84]

Specialist Christopher Wayne Sawyer, twenty-nine, was discovered "unresponsive" (after allegedly shooting himself in the head) at his residence on base on March 5, 2020. A native of Longview, Washington, Sawyer had reportedly witnessed repeated acts of sexual harassment and encouraged the victims (male and female) to file reports, sometimes accompanying them or filing corroborating accounts. Nicknamed "The Governor" by members of his unit, Sawyer stood six feet, five inches tall and weighed just over 230 pounds and reportedly wasn't comfortable ignoring the maltreatment that some of his fellow soldiers experienced or bashful about expressing his contempt. He had a five-year-old daughter at home and was so shocked by some of the behavior at Fort Cavazos that he was anxious to leave. According to Sawyer's wife, Destanie, he and others said little was done about most of the harassment and when the files and complaints climbed the ranks, they were swept under the rug.[85]

Then, Sawyer himself was swept under the rug.

On March 14, 2020, Specialist Freddy Beningo Delacruz Jr. was gunned down with two others at Summerlyn Apartments in Killeen. A twenty-three-year-old native of Vidalia, Georgia, Delacruz was shot seven times in the back; his girlfriend (pregnant with his child) was found on her bathroom floor, having been shot seven times; and Delacruz's friend, veteran Shaquan Markell, was shot execution-style on the living room couch, a video game controller in his lap. Twenty-three-year-old Barnard Lnell Morrow, a

Houston native Vanessa Guillen was murdered with a hammer, physically dismembered and buried in a shallow grave after sexual harassment claims in 2020. *Public domain.*

former soldier from Mississippi—and a man who considered his victims "family"—was charged with triple homicide and convicted of their murders in the spring of 2022.

On April 23, 2020, twenty-year-old Houston native Vanessa Guillen was reported missing after telling her family she was being sexually harassed by a fellow soldier. Her remains were found in a shallow grave near the Leon River more than two months later, on June 30. She had been dismembered and partially encased in concrete by twenty-year-old Specialist Aaron Davis Robinson of Calumet, Illinois. Robinson had bludgeoned Guillen to death and then enlisted the help of his girlfriend, twenty-four-year-old Cecily Anne Aguilar (the estranged wife of another Fort Cavazos soldier), to help him conceal the crime. When Robinson found out Guillen's remains had been discovered, he fled, killing himself with a handgun before he could be cornered by Killeen police. Aguilar pleaded guilty in U.S. Magistrate Court in Waco to one count of being an accessory after the fact and three counts of making false statements to the government.

The day Guillen was reported missing, twenty-one-year-old Private Gavin Chambers died at Fort Cavazos. Six days later, on April 29, 2020, nineteen-year-old Private Joshua Holden Barnwell reportedly died after an "accidental weapons discharge" struck him in the head.

On May 16, 2020, Sergeant Brad Reynolds, thirty-seven, committed suicide, leaving behind a wife, two sons and a daughter. Private First Class Brandon Scott Rosencrans was found dead on the side of a road in Harker Heights (near Killeen) two days later. He had been shot four times at close range after befriending and then apparently being drugged by thirty-year-old Brandon Michael Olivares and thirty-nine-year-old Estrellita Hidalgo Falcon. Rosencrans's jeep was found burning three miles from his body. Falcon was sentenced to nineteen months for auto theft. Olivares was charged with murder and accepted a plea deal from Bell County in late March 2023. He will spend the next forty years in prison.

Staff Sergeant Richard Lee Harrington Jr., forty-five, of Brooklyn, New York, killed himself on May 25, 2020. Sergeant Harrington's suicide was followed by that of twenty-three-year-old Specialist James Green.

Sergeant Geraldo Andre Mora-Cruz was found "unresponsive" at Fort Cavazos (formerly Fort Hood) on March 15, 2015. *Public domain.*

The skeletal remains of Private Second Class Gregory Scott Morales were found in a Killeen field on June 19, 2020, ten months after the twenty-four-year-old Sapulpa, Oklahoma native was reported missing.

Navajo citizen Specialist Miguel D. Yazzie died at Fort Cavazos on July 3, 2020, but his cause of death was not provided. Twenty-six-year-old Private Mejhor Morta of Pensacola, Florida, was found unresponsive on July 17, 2020, after drowning in nearby Stillhouse Hollow Lake.[86] Local fishermen discovered his body at the base of a dam. Specialist Francisco Gilberto Hernandez-Vargas of Woodside, New York—in the same battalion as Morta—was found dead in the water at Stillhouse Hollow Lake on August 2, 2020. The twenty-four-year-old had reportedly been riding on an inflatable tube being pulled by a boat before he died.

Then, on August 25, 2020, Sergeant Elder Fernandez of Brockton, Massachusetts, was found hanging from a tree in Temple, about twenty-five miles from Fort Cavazos. A preliminary autopsy ruled Fernandez's death a suicide, but it came not long after he reported to his superiors and his family that he was being harassed and that one of his commanding officers had sexually assaulted him. He was hospitalized for psychiatric care at the on-base Carl R. Darnall Army Medical Center in mid-August and disappeared the day he was released.

Navajo citizen Private Corlton Chee became the twenty-eighth soldier to die at Fort Cavazos in 2020, on September 2. He reportedly collapsed during a training exercise.

"OPERATION UNRESPONSIVE" RAN AT a steady clip at Fort Cavazos for at least a decade, but the campaign was abridged in December 2020, when numerous Fort Cavazos leaders were found to be permissive of sexual harassment and assault and were relieved of command or suspended. Especially damning was the army review determination that "no commanding general or subordinate senior commander proactively intervened to mitigate 'known risks of high crime, sexual assault and sexual harassment.'"[87]

Will Fort Cavazos have our soldiers backs any better than Fort Hood did? *Courtesy of Sergeant. Ken Scar, public domain, via Wikimedia Commons.*

In the last couple of years, victims' friends and family members have claimed that "The Good Place" base gives off a "bad vibe," warning journalists like May Jeong not to be out around Fort Cavazos after dark and to be on the lookout for "cartels."[88]

Cartels. In Central Texas.

IN THE MARCH 27, 2023 edition of Military.com, former U.S. Army veteran Lucy Del Gaudio was succinct and to the point: "What type of place fosters a climate that makes individuals want to take their own lives? What type of homicides are taking place within a military installation?"

Several of our fellow Texans participated in the attack on the U.S. Capitol on January 6, 2021. Many of our fellow Texans have patrolled our border with Mexico wary of external threats. And plenty of Texas politicians continue to discuss secession.

Who's watching Fort Cavazos?

I limited my examination of the mayhem and carnage at Fort Cavazos to 2020—one year. But the trend continued into 2022, ending with a twenty-six-year-old Skiatook, Oklahoma native named Justin Lambillotte reportedly committing suicide in his barracks on December 23.[89] Fort Cavazos has been a disturbing new chapter of the Wild West for over a decade, and right under our noses at that. It's also been an asinine model of good ol' boy abuses (and excuses) right in front of our eyes. And Fort Cavazos clearly seems to have been more dangerous for the soldiers stationed there than any current combat zone they might be sent to.

I WROTE ABOUT THE subject again in the March 29, 2023 edition of *Fort Worth Weekly*—a Metro piece based on this chapter of *Tell-Tale Texas*. I said, "Though I applaud the decision to rename Fort Hood after General Richard Cavazos, if I was a member of the Cavazos family, I might be having second thoughts. It would be a shame to lend a real patriot's name to a chronically fubar military base in a state governed by often conspicuously unpatriotic leaders."

I sent the original draft to my editor on March 16, 2023. On Friday, March 24, 2023, base officials announced that Fort Hood would officially be renamed Fort Cavazos on May 9, 2023. And it was.

Coincidence? Or just good timing?

Fort Cavazos owns it all, now, regardless.

CRITICAL RACE LEERY

Despite denials, selective memory or cultural amnesia, there is little doubt that the community of Slocum is aware of its frightful past and endeavors mightily to transcend it even while refusing to acknowledge it. But silence is not the proper course of action for Slocum or Anderson County or the State of Texas. The Slocum Massacre will not remain buried.
—E.R. Bills, *The 1910 Slocum Massacre: An Act of Genocide in East Texas*

When you decide to investigate something, especially on a controversial topic, you try to get the facts straight. You try to perform due diligence. The last thing you want is for your effort to miss the mark or leave any stone unturned. Sometimes, however, it happens.

Then what?

Then this.

TEN YEARS AGO, I wrote a story about an act of genocide in East Texas. It was titled "Town's 1910 Racial Strife a Nearly Forgotten Piece of Texas Past," and it appeared in the February 22, 2013 *Austin American-Statesman*. In the days and weeks that followed, I was contacted by Christen Thompson of The History Press, and she offered me a book deal.

I'd never written a book. I'd never even thought about writing a book. I was reticent, to say the least.

First, I didn't know if I was capable of writing a book. Second, no one had ever written a book on the subject, and I wasn't sure there was enough information available to even complete such a book. Third, the subject involved a massacre of innocent Blacks—and I am a white man. I thought that surely some Black graduate student or academic was pursuing it.

I researched the subject on the internet. I perused pertinent scholarly journals online. I couldn't find anything. I told Miss Thompson, who is also white, that I wasn't sure I was the right person to write the book. She pointed out that I'd already written about the pogrom for a major newspaper, and it was honest and well received. She wasn't wrong.

The "1910 Racial Strife" piece attracted the attention of some of the descendants of the Rosewood Massacre in Florida. That 1923 massacre had already received film treatment, but they approached me about writing about it. I politely told them that I didn't feel comfortable with covering something that happened so far away, in another state, and I thanked them for their interest. I was then contacted by a descendant of someone who was involved in the carnage I'd written about in the *Statesman*. Not a descendant of a Black victim, but an ashamed descendant of one of the white perpetrators.[90]

The book that I wound up writing about this atrocity was *The 1910 Slocum Massacre: An Act of Genocide in East Texas*.

BY THE EARLY TWENTIETH century in the Slocum area of southeastern Anderson County, several Black citizens were considerably propertied, a few owning stores, businesses and other establishments. The Reconstruction period after the Civil War was over, and some African Americans, previously born into slavery, had established footholds in the local economy. The Holley and Wilson families, for example, apparently owned one of the community's only general stores and hundreds of acres of rich farmland.

This alone, in parts of the South, would have been grounds for white violence. But in the Slocum area, which included the small communities of Percilla (Houston County), Alderbranch, Denson Springs and the "negro colonies" of St. James and Sandy Beulah, there were other issues. In early May 1910, a white regional road-construction foreman named Enoch Williams put Abe Wilson (the Wilson partner of the local general store and related to the Holleys by marriage) in charge of rounding up help for local road improvements. A white half-renter named Jim Spurger was infuriated. On May 20 or May 23, Spurger showed up for road repairs with a gun and refused

Galveston native Jack
Johnson defeated the
"Great White Hope,"
Jim Jeffries, in early
July 1910 to remain
the world heavyweight
boxing champion.
Wikipedia Commons.

to help. He contributed one dollar for the day's work and said he would join
the effort "when we get a white man for an overseer." At a Juneteenth picnic
on June 19, 1910, a white man named Reddin Alford troubled Marsh Holley
over a bank note, and frustrations lingered. The following day, a Black man
named Leonard Johnson was seized from the sheriff of the next county over
(Cherokee County) by a mob of 150 white men and burned at the stake—no
trial, no jury—for the alleged rape of a seventeen-year-old white girl named
Maudie Redden. And several Cherokee County Blacks who believed Johnson
was innocent "were beaten," "otherwise harshly treated" and, according to
some accounts, murdered by the mob.

Then, when Black Galveston native Jack Johnson pummeled the "Great
White Hope," Jim Jeffries, to remain the world heavyweight boxing champion
in early July 1910, many whites construed the pride that Johnson's victory
inspired in African Americans as "uppity" behavior.

Jim Spurger began openly fomenting white discontent. Wild rumors began to circulate suggesting that local Blacks were planning an uprising. Racist malcontents manipulated the local white population.

On Wednesday, July 27, 1910, Abe Wilson's house was burned to the ground. And by Friday, July 29, 1910, white hysteria had transmogrified into a cold-blooded, murderous white rampage.

Goaded by Spurger and others, hundreds of white citizens from Anderson County and the surrounding counties converged on the Slocum area armed with pistols, shotguns and rifles. That morning, near Sadlers Creek, they fired on three young African Americans headed to feed cattle, killing eighteen-year-old Cleveland Larkin and wounding fifteen-year-old Charlie Wilson. The third, eighteen-year-old Lusk Holley, escaped, only to be shot at again later in the day while he, his twenty-year-old brother Alex and their friend William Foreman were fleeing to Palestine. Alex was killed, and Lusk was wounded. Foreman ran for his life. Lusk pretended to be dead so that a group of twenty white men wouldn't finish him off.

For the next two days, white mobs reportedly marched through the area gunning down an unknown number of Black Texans. A thirty-year-old African American named John Hays was found dead in a roadway, and twenty-year-old Sam Baker was shot to death in Dick Wilson's house. Dick Wilson (Charlie Wilson's father), his son Geffy and seventy-year-old Ben Dancy were killed while sitting with the body the following day.

In addition to the Anderson County murders, which occurred near the county line, Will Burley was killed just south of the line in Houston County. And he wasn't the only one. According to contemporary newspaper accounts, white mobs traveled from house to house in Anderson and Houston Counties, shooting African Americans who answered their hails and slaughtering more while they tended their fields.

Almost every early newspaper report (in the *New York Times*, *Galveston Daily News*, *Fort Worth Star-Telegram*, et al.) on the transpiring bloodshed in and around Slocum portrayed the African-Americans as the aggressors, indicating that the local white community was simply defending itself. These accounts were gross mischaracterizations. When Anderson County district judge Benjamin H. Gardner closed saloons in Palestine and ordered local gun and ammunition stores to stop selling their wares on July 30, it was not to stop a Black uprising; it was to defuse what the *Galveston Daily News* called an indescribable, one-sided "reign of terror" characterized by "a fierce manhunt in the woods" and resulting in bullet-riddled Black bodies everywhere.

Former slave Jack Holley would become and remain a successful Black businessman until the Slocum Massacre in southeastern Anderson County in 1910. *Courtesy of Constance Hollie-Jawaid.*

When reporters gathered on July 31, up to two dozen murders had been reported and dozens more were suspected, but local authorities had collected only eight bodies. Once the carnage began, hundreds of African Americans had fled to the surrounding piney woods and local marshes. And by the time the Texas Rangers and state militia arrived, there was no way to estimate the number of African American dead.

On August 1, a few Texas Rangers and some locals gathered up several bodies of African Americans and buried them (wrapped in blankets and placed in a single large box) in a large pit four miles south of Slocum. Some reports suggest the unmarked mass grave was full of dozens of corpses, because law enforcement personnel kept coming back out of the woods with more bodies. Farther north, Marsh Holley was found on a road just south of Palestine. He begged the authorities for help, requesting that he be taken to the county jail for his own protection.

AFTER THE FIRST SEVERAL murders, most members of the African American community began fleeing, but this didn't stop the white mobs. Most of the victims were shot in the back. Two bodies found near the former town of Percilla (in Houston County) still had travel bundles of food and clothing at their sides.

Anderson County sheriff William H. Black said it would be "difficult to find out just how many [Blacks] were killed," because they were "scattered all over the woods." He also admitted that buzzards would find many of the victims first.

With the arrival of the press—and after the failure of early attempts to spin the news reports to portray the African American victims as armed insurrectionists—the guilty parties clearly engaged in damage control. Some of the transgressors returned to the murder scenes to remove the evidence of their crimes. Some threatened potential witnesses and fellow perpetrators if they "crawfished."[91] But regarding the official narrative, Sheriff Black was unequivocal. "Men were going about killing Negroes as fast as they could

Of the Slocum Massacre, Anderson County sheriff W.H. Black said, "Men were going about killing Negroes as fast as they could find them, and, so far as I was able to ascertain, without any real cause." *Wikipedia Commons*.

find them," he told the *New York Times*. "And, so far as I was able to ascertain, without any real cause."

"These Negroes have done no wrong that I can discover," Black continued. "I don't know how many [whites] were in the mob, but there may have been 200 or 300. Some of them cut telephone wires. They hunted the Negroes down like sheep."

According to the local law enforcement leaders on hand at the time, eight casualties was a conservative number. Sheriff Black and others insisted that there were at least a dozen more; some reports suggest there may have been dozens if not hundreds more. Some witnesses counted twenty-two casualties. Elkhart native F.M. Power said there were thirty "missing negroes." Slocum-area resident Luther Hardeman claimed to have knowledge of eighteen African American casualties—that's the original number reported by the *Galveston Daily News* and the *New York Times* (on July 31)—but the body count seemed to shrink as the pogrom's publicity grew.

When a *Galveston Daily News* correspondent visited Lusk Holley and Charlie Wilson on July 31, they were still suffering from the gunshot wounds they had received. The writer reported that their injuries would be "relieved only by death unless medical attention is speedily afforded." Wilson had a broken leg, damage to one ankle and "glancing wounds through his chest." Holley had eight to ten pieces of buckshot in his lower left abdominal area and damage to one arm. Physicians had perfunctorily treated their wounds when they were first discovered two days prior, but not since.

Wilson told the *Galveston Daily News* correspondent that he had recognized two of the assailants during the first shooting on July 29. Holley said that after he had been wounded in the second shooting later in the day, a different group of white men had come upon him while he pretended to be dead. He said he recognized the voice of a prominent local farmer named Jeff Wise, who deemed his apparent death and his brother's actual death "a shame" as he passed by.

The corpses of Black victims scattered all over the area were being disposed of, and the perpetrators of the bloodlust were making themselves scarce, so Judge Gardner made a tough decision. Instead of waiting for the gunsmoke to clear, he decided to arrest the suspects he could and charge them with the murders that could be immediately prosecuted—before all the evidence and more of the suspects disappeared.

At the initial grand jury hearing, a large percentage of the remaining Slocum residents were subpoenaed; some residents refused to testify and were arrested. Judge Gardner told the all-male, all-white jury that the massacre was "a disgrace, not only to the county, but to the state," and it was up to them to do their "full duty."

According to the August 2 edition of the *Palestine Daily Herald*, Judge Gardner attempted to clarify the charges and the issues at hand, explaining various statutes to the jury. He specifically noted that even if there had been threats or conspiracies "on the part of any number of Negroes to do violence to white persons, it would not justify" vigilantism. "The law furnishes ample remedy," Gardner continued. "There is no justification for shooting men in the back, waylaying or killing them in their houses."

When the grand jury findings were reported on August 17, several hundred witnesses had been examined. Though eleven men were initially arrested, seven were finally indicted: Isom Garner, B.J. Jenkins, Steve Jenkins, Andrew Kirkwood, Henry Shipper, Curtis Spurger and Jim Spurger. Only Kirkwood was immediately granted bail. Another man, Alvin Oliver, turned state's evidence. Two cases moved forward, one based on killings in Anderson County and one involving the murder of Will Burley in Houston County. No one was ever indicted in the deaths of John Hays or Alex Holley, and no other victims were ever reported.

In the weeks and months following what came to be known as the Slocum Massacre, the local Black residents made a mass exodus, leaving homes, properties and businesses behind. That was fine with the white perpetrators, whether they were participants or bystanders.

On November 14, 1910, the defendants in the Houston County case (Jim Spurger, Isom Garner, Andrew Kirkwood, William Henry, B.J. Jenkins and Henry Shipper) were arraigned, and each entered a plea of not guilty to the charge of first-degree murder. The presiding judge denied bail to every defendant except Shipper. His bail was set at $5,000, and his family and friends—including Thomas F.L. Hassell,[92] whose relative Floyd Hassell would later recuse himself from the official Frank J. Robinson murder/ suicide inquest—put up their lands and properties as his surety.

On Wednesday, December 12, the defendants in the Anderson County case were arraigned, and Judge Gardner, on his own motion, announced that the trial venue would be changed to Limestone County unless the attorneys for both the state and the defendants agreed to a different location in the counties of Navarro, McLennan, Williamson, Travis or Harris.

Gardner preferred Navarro County, but the attorneys for the state and the defendants agreed on a venue in Harris County. This was fortuitous for the defendants. The front-page *Houston Post* headline after Jack Johnson defeated Jim Jeffries read, "Ebon Gloom Loomed Deep as Negro Trounced Jeff," and the lede was quite telling:

> *The ebon complexion of the world's champion had nothing on the gloom that settled over Houston yesterday after the flash came that Johnson had knocked out the white man. The gloom settled down in such large squares, oblong and chunks as to be almost opaque.*

And if you think that was an exaggeration of white despair (and desperation), consider this clip in the *Honey Grove Signal* three-and-a-half weeks later, on the day the violence began in the Slocum area:

> *Suppose a South African Gorilla had come over to the United States, put on store clothes, walked up to Jim Jeffries and demanded a fight. Would Jeffries have displayed any brains by recognizing him? He would have said to the gorilla: "You are not in my class. I shall keep my part of American sport in the human family." And that's exactly what he should have said to the big sifter footed, liver-lipped, burr-head who paralyzed him and pulverized him at Reno the other day.*
>
> *The Lord knows the negro race was impudent enuf* [sic] *prior to the Johnson victory at Reno. You can scarcely pick up a newspaper without reading where some negro has been mobbed for his meanness. There are a lot of cerulean bellied yankee aristocrats who insist on referring to the coon as "Mistah" and the coon forthwith proceeds to rape some white woman or little girl. As long as the negro was a slave, he was harmless, for he realized that there was a great gaping hiatus yawning between himself and the white race and he cheerfully kept his post. The old "befo de wah" slave nigger had no more notion of breeding with a white woman than a monkey would breeding with a swan.*[93]

Appalling, yes. But to be fair, Honey Grove sits between Bonham, Texas— where local whites and lawyers pilfered the massive land bequeathment of Thomas Bean from his extended Black family in multiple litigious scams during the latter part of the nineteenth and early part of the twentieth centuries[94]—and Paris, Texas, where at least four Black men were burned at the stake between the Civil War era and 1920.[95] But the citizens of Honey Grove—which today bills itself as "The Sweetest Town in Texas"—did burn their own Black man at the stake in mid-May 1930.

This indirectly draws our attention back to the lynching of Leonard Johnson, just two weeks before Jack Johnson "pulverized" Jim Jeffries. The seventeen-year-old white female whom Johnson was accused of assaulting and murdering was the daughter of W.H. Redden, the constable for Precinct 6 of Cherokee County, and Johnson was actually a "county convict working off a crime" at Constable Redden's place. According the *Palestine Daily Herald*, "the negro was suspicioned and arrested, and the evidence was sufficient to warrant the mob in reaching the conclusion that the right man was arrested, though he stoutly maintained his innocence."[96] The lynch mob reportedly overpowered Sheriff C.K. Norwood and ten deputies. Then, several African Americans in the community got wind of what was happening and attempted to intervene and, again, were beaten and in some cases killed.

Should I mention that the white mob went to a lot of trouble to avoid due process?

Should I also mention that Johnson was still working Constable Redden's land when he was arrested? So, if the mob and the *Palestine Daily Herald* got it straight, Johnson returned to his work after the rape and murder to fulfil the terms of his convict labor agreement?

IN EARLY MAY 1911, attorney Ned R. Morris of Palestine successfully petitioned the state's Court of Criminal Appeals to grant bail for the defendants. Eventually, all those charged were released on $1,500 bail, and none of the indictments were ever prosecuted.

Meanwhile, the personal holdings of many Slocum-area white citizens increased handsomely.

The abandoned African American properties were absorbed or repurposed as the white population saw fit. Many Black landowners were either dead or missing, and their land titles were vacated or revised. And then a fire at the Anderson County courthouse conveniently destroyed many of the original titles, so the revisions couldn't be examined or questioned.

A racial pogrom and the resultant racial expulsion. An opportunistic white land grab. Possibly several unmarked mass graves still unverified and unexhumed today. A reprehensible act of genocide conspicuously absent from Texas memory.

THE STRANGE THING ABOUT the Slocum Massacre piece I'd written in the *Austin American-Statesman* in February 2013 was that I was actually researching another racial pogrom in West Texas when I accidentally stumbled on the Slocum atrocity. I was looking for internet information on the 1918 Porvenir Massacre and kept seeing mentions of a "race riot" in East Texas a few years before. I'd never heard of or learned about either in school or college but was pretty far along in my research on the Porvenir Massacre when I took a closer look at the Slocum Massacre. It shocked me.

I'd seen *Mississippi Burning* and *Rosewood* and had even heard about the Tulsa Race Massacre, but I wasn't aware that anything like that had happened in Texas. And as I perused and scrutinized the reports of the carnage in the Slocum area of East Texas, I realized that something was amiss. The reporting didn't make sense. The numbers didn't add up.

Hundreds of white men rode and/or marched around southeastern Anderson County and northeastern Houston County (Percilla, Augusta, etc.)—after emptying the local gun and ammunition stores—reportedly shooting their Black neighbors on sight. And only eight casualties?

Left to right: E.R. Bills, Constance Hollie-Jawaid and Carolyn Phillips standing at the Slocum Massacre historical marker on the day of its dedication. *Courtesy of Paul Beatty.*

The harder I looked, the more suspicious I became. I subscribed to a newspaper archive. I discovered that a local *Star-Telegram* writer, Tim Madigan, had written about the massacre in 2011. His work led to Texas House of Representatives Resolution 865 on March 30, 2011 (HR 865, filed by Representatives Marc Veasey and Lon Burnam on March 11, 2011). It officially acknowledged the Slocum Massacre.

I picked Madigan's brain. I asked for information on his sources. But after Madigan's stories and HR 865, his sources didn't have much to say. I suspected they faced reprisals.

I accepted a book deal with The History Press, but one book became two. I asked Thompson if I could write a collection of obscure Texas stories first and publish a book on the Slocum Massacre after. The collection of stories—originally titled *Texas Curiosities*—became *Texas Obscurities: Stories of the Peculiar, Exceptional and Nefarious*, and it includes chapters on the Slocum and Porvenir Massacres. It was published just eight months after the Slocum Massacre piece in the *Statesman*.

My book on the Slocum Massacre itself appeared just six months later, on May 12, 2014.

TWO BOOKS IN FOURTEEN months published six months apart, and that after a virtual standing start.

I didn't know any better.

I worked on the Slocum Massacre book while I was finishing *Texas Obscurities* but immediately encountered frustrating obstacles. The first descendant of the Holley family (now spelled Hollie), who I contacted to interview, referred me to a Fort Worth preacher who served as the family spokesperson. When I got him on the phone and explained that I was trying to do a book on the Slocum Massacre and needed to speak with members of the Hollie family for details and background, he had just one question: "How much?"

I futilely explained that I was a freelance writer who drove a seven-year-old Nissan Frontier, was not paid a book advance, was clearly not trying to write a book that might make a fortune (à la *Harry Potter* or *Twilight*), had never even published a book before and was not rich or even well off. Our conversation ended succinctly but not impolitely.

I was off to a bad start, and things grew markedly worse.

Denied access to the Hollie family, I reached out to the Anderson County Historical Commission. I got commission chair Jimmy Ray Odom on the horn, and when he heard what I was initially inquiring about, he was very keen on making sure I wasn't a member of the NAACP. I assured him I wasn't. "I don't truck with those folks," he said. "They were here complaining about the Confederate flag at our courthouse awhile back." I reassured him I wasn't a member, and he proceeded to explain to me how there was never any real evidence supporting the notion that there was a massacre in Slocum, and that the hoax was based on exaggerated newspaper reports from outside the region. I demurred and insisted I'd seen local reports detailing the bloodshed as well. We went back and forth briefly, Odom denying and me pressing. Then he got real quiet. He wasn't getting anywhere with me, so, after a long pause, he asked me straight out, "Aren't you a white man?"

I was somewhat taken aback, but I recovered quickly. "Yes," I said. "But I'm also a human being, and the folks who died in the Slocum Massacre were human beings." Odom didn't respond.

"I'm gonna tell this story," I continued, "whether y'all help me or not."

"Not" turned out to be the case, but I caught some breaks. I found a junior college research paper tucked in a "Black History" or "Slocum" file at the Palestine Public Library. It gave me more detail and listed other sources. It made me aware of Felix Green's book *The Piersons and Barnetts of East Texas*, which includes mentions of the massacre and family victims affected by it. I then realized that the massacre had spread into Houston County. I camped out in the Houston County court archives and then visited the Houston County Historical Commission in person.

The county chairperson was a Black woman named Barbara Wooten, and when I informed her what I was interested in looking into, she was skeptical. But once she realized I was on the up-and-up, she gave me access to a cache of theretofore unpublished correspondence, which helped me finish the book.

THE PUBLICATION OF *THE 1910 Slocum Massacre: An Act of Genocide in East Texas* turned out to be just the beginning. When Constance Hollie-Jawaid, the chief spokesperson for the descendants of the Slocum Massacre, became aware of the book and read it, she called me on the verge of tears. She was surprised by how much of the story she hadn't been aware of and then became furious at the family spokesman who had discouraged me from speaking with her and the rest of the family.

Subsequently, Hollie-Jawaid asked me to assist her in applying for a Slocum Massacre historical marker. She sponsored the effort, and I helped her write the application. When Hollie-Jawaid submitted the application to the Anderson County Historical Commission, Odom was immediately hostile. He criticized our application, variously claiming it was unprofessional, based on rumors, antagonistic and, finally, too focused on negative rather than positive history. Then Odom claimed the commission didn't have a quorum and wasn't going to consider applications that year. After that, he insisted that the commission would have considered the application but that I had put Hollie-Jawaid up to historical marker application to increase the sales of my book at an Anderson County pioneer festival that neither Constance nor I had ever heard of.

Odom obviously didn't know Constance Hollie-Jawaid very well.

When she had had enough of the Anderson County Historical Commission's machinations, she appealed directly to the Texas State Historical Association. Its members agreed to consider the application independent of the county historical commission. We were off to the races (pardon the pun).

During the Slocum Massacre historical marker application process, forces from every side of the effort tried to dissuade or divide us. Some of my white friends and associates accused me of being ashamed of my whiteness. Some of Hollie-Jawaid's Black friends and associates believed she shouldn't be pursuing justice for the Slocum Massacre with a white man.

With the date of a decision on Texas historical markers approaching in January 2015, Hollie-Jawaid and I were beset from every direction with criticism and predictions of failure. Our white detractors acted like it was an assault on the republic itself; some of our Black detractors also condemned it outright or told us it would not be approved without their support.

Constance Hollie-Jawaid ignored them all, and, on January 29, 2015, the state historical commission unanimously approved the Slocum Massacre historical marker application with a score of ninety-eight on a one-hundred-point scale. When the marker was placed and dedicated on January 16, 2016, it became the first State of Texas historical marker to specifically acknowledge racial violence against African Americans.

Tireless educator Constance Hollie-Jawaid is a descendant of victims of the 1910 Slocum Massacre and the chief progenitor of the historical marker commemorating the atrocity. *Photo by author.*

Hollie-Jawaid and I were elated and, on some level, relieved. But we both knew there was still work to be done. Over the next several years we tried again and again to bring attention to the unmarked mass graves in news reports and features. We visited the Slocum Massacre historical marker on the July 29 anniversary of the atrocity every year, one of us or the other, or both, usually with other members of the Hollie and Wilson families.

After the marker effort was approved, I think we both thought things would settle down and we could focus on other stuff and our families. And we did. But the Slocum Massacre and its victims never went away. The specters of Hollie-Jawaid's ancestors literally and figuratively never stopped haunting us.

In the decade since my feature on the Slocum Massacre was published, we have corroborated on two screenplays based on the Slocum pogrom,[97] and they both have been optioned, but neither have been produced.

Every year or two, another journalist, filmmaker or playwright approaches us with ideas about a compelling filmic, stage or radio production, but nothing ever comes of it. We have become cynical. We are exhausted.

But a positive note appeared near the end of 2022.

ON PAGE NINETY-TWO OF *The 1910 Slocum Massacre: An Act of Genocide in East Texas*, I mention that the remaining five defendants in Anderson County district judge Benjamin Gardner's initial, still unprosecuted indictments filed a writ of habeas corpus at the Court of Criminal Appeals in Travis County. It was early May 1911, and they were still incarcerated and being held without bail. I suspect Gardner knew there was little hope of their being successfully prosecuted and meted out what legal complications he could in lieu of the justice he was doubtful that the victims of the Slocum Massacre would ever receive. He was eventually proven right. Jim Spurger, B.J. Jenkins, S.C. Jenkins, Curtis Spurger and Isom Garner were each granted a $1,500 bail and, after posting it, walked away free men. They were never tried in a court of law and were never prosecuted or punished for their crimes.

They weren't the only ones, of course, just the most inconvenienced. Judge Gardner did what he could while he could, but dozens of the perpetrators of the Slocum Massacre were never arrested or charged, and dozens if not hundreds of the victims lost their lives and their property.

My father, E.R. Bills Sr., died while I was finishing my book on the Slocum Massacre, and I dedicated the book to him. On November 10, 2022—a day that

In 2016, veteran NPR and Texas Public Radio journalist David Martin Davies received an Edward R. Murrow Award for Best News Documentary for "Should Texas Remember or Forget the Slocum Massacre?" *Photo by Davies.*

would have marked my father's eightieth birthday—I received an email from Dr. Steven A. Reich of James Madison University in Harrisonburg, Virginia. I learned that my research on the Slocum Massacre had been incomplete. I'd dug around in the Anderson and Houston County courthouse archives and found notes and basic proceedings on the cases against a few of the white folks behind the Slocum Massacre, but I'd never come across actual testimony, and I—in my haste or inexperience—failed to check the Texas State Library and Archive Commission for the State Court of Criminal Appeals records. Dr. Reich, however, did, and he reached out to me.

> *My research has unearthed records from the criminal proceedings, including the full transcript of the March 1911 bail hearing that lasted ten days. The more than 350 pages of sworn testimony from fifty-four witnesses, Black and white, offers a window onto the Black community, the massacre, its perpetrators, and its victims. It allows us to reconstruct the massacre—at least the killing of six of the known victims—with considerable precision. Even if the white people of Anderson County kept the crimes of their forefathers quiet for more than a hundred years, their ancestors spoke on record about what happened. And their words have remained preserved in those*

court papers. Furthermore, the black witnesses offer compelling testimony, on public record, about what happened to them and who pulled the triggers that killed their family members. The document reveals a remarkable effort by Black teenagers, women, and men to act politically with incredible courage to compel civil authorities to acknowledge and denounce the violence that visited their community.

I was dumbstruck at first and then mightily frustrated. I'd missed something—something that would have been incredibly useful in Constance Hollie-Jawaid's and my skirmishes with the Anderson County Historical Commission, et al.

I had to find it and see it for myself. Dr. Reich sent me excerpts and gave me a few clues, but not the entire record. I located it immediately and ordered my own copy. Some of the surviving Black victims actually testified against the white defendants before a judge, even pointing out and identifying them at the time. In *Ex Parte Jim Sperger* [sic] *et al.*, forty witnesses testified for the state, and sixteen testified for the defendants.

CHARLIE WILSON IDENTIFIED ISOM Garner as the man who shot him[98] and identified him in court. Will Burley's wife, Ermie, testified and identified Jim Spurger as the man who murdered her unarmed husband on their front porch.[99] Dick Wilson's wife, Margaret, testified that Spurger and Andrew Jenkins murdered Sam Baker after finding him in a room at her house on July 29; she also testified that Isom Garner shot her son Geffy, that Steve Jenkins shot her husband, that Dick and Curtis Spurger shot Ben Dancy—and she identified them in court.[100]

Abe Wilson—whom several of the white witnesses for the state and the defense testified that the whites in the community were afraid of—testified that after his house was shot up and burned, his prospects in the Slocum area were nil.

I left that neighborhood because I couldn't stay there without being killed, and I thought I had better leave. I wasn't so scared as all that, but I didn't want to have to have so much trouble if I could get around it....I don't enjoy having trouble with white folks or anybody else.[101]

It's hard not to be heartened and impressed by the courage of these victims, especially taking the stand and identifying some of the perpetrators of the bloodshed at a time when—as many have suggested—no white man had ever been convicted of killing a Black man in Texas. Also incredible in the record, especially looking back, is how the defense team's witnesses practically made the prosecution's case for them. Here are excerpts from some of the testimony:

> *"I heard about the burning of that negro in Cherokee County, and I noticed the change in the negroes at that time. It seemed like to me it made the negroes worse; insolent and mean and impudent; more impudent than they had ever been before."*
>
> *"The negroes didn't seem to be as quiet as they had been, and it seemed like they carried their guns more frequently."*
>
> *"They were bigoted and sassy among some white people."*
>
> *"And I noticed about their conduct after the Jack Johnson fight, and they would call each other Jack Johnson and say 'well, you know, a negro is stouter than anybody else, and is more of a man.'"*
>
> *"...I met several of them in the road and they didn't speak to me, and I didn't think they acted very polite. I have seen them pass by whistling and talking and going on just like they didn't care. That is what I call a bigoted person."*
>
> *"I remember the trouble they had down there near Slocum when the darkies were killed. I think the first darkies was killed on Friday; that is what I heard, but I don't know only from what I heard...that the negroes were up to some devilment."*
>
> *"The negroes down there are not disbehaving now."*

After reading the entire record, I realized what I'd missed.

A game changer.

Certainly bad news for chronic sufferers of white fragility and white denial in Anderson County and across the state. But it is also bleak for conservative politicians, the regressive Texas legislature and the delusional critics of critical race theory.

In the next decade or so, not just a historical marker but also a full-blown, state-funded monument—not unlike those standing to commemorate the victims of the Tulsa Race Massacre in Oklahoma, the Rosewood Massacre in Florida and the Elaine Massacre in Arkansas—will be standing in East Texas.

And it's somewhat ironic.

The rights and privileges that so many Texans have been complaining about losing in the previous decade are the same rights and privileges white conservatives were allowed to kill Black people for seeking or simply enjoying in 1910. My original *Statesman* article on the Slocum Massacre was just a clumsy start. But these firsthand, eyewitness court documents provide us with the indisputable proof.

NOTES

Chapter 1

1. Texas Public Radio reporter David Martin Davies and I interviewed Alexander Nemer on July 31, 2022.
2. The police chief's homicide conclusion was reported by the *Palestine Daily Herald*, the *Austin American-Statesman*, et al.
3. *Palestine Daily Herald*, October 15, 1976.
4. *Austin American-Statesman*, October 21, 1976.
5. *Dallas Morning News*, October 20, 1976.
6. Dorothy Robinson agreed with this conclusion during remarks to *Dallas Morning News* (October 24, 1976).
7. *Austin American-Statesman*, October 20, 1976.
8. Civil Action No. TY-73-VA-236, *Frank J. Robinson, Rodney Howard and Timothy Smith vs. Commissioners Court, Anderson County, and N.R. Link, County Judge, Anderson County*.
9. To claim that Robinson, Smith and Howard's successful litigation to end local gerrymandering—the most visible progenitor of which was Robinson—didn't suggest motive arguably strains credulity.
10. This was flattering, of course. But *Texas Monthly* was the first media outlet to which I pitched a feature on the assassination of Frank J. Robinson back in October 2015. I never got a response from the editor in chief, deputy editor or a senior editor.

11. A few years back, a local retired law enforcement officer had access to the images as well but wouldn't allow me access.
12. *Austin American-Statesman*, October 21, 1976.
13. Ibid., October 21, 1976.
14. *Denton Record-Chronicle*, October 29, 1976.
15. George Thomas "Mickey" Leland III (November 27, 1944–August 7, 1989) was an antipoverty activist who later became a Democratic congressman from the Texas Eighteenth District and chair of the Congressional Black Caucus. He died in a plane crash on a mission trip in Ethiopia on August 7, 1989.

Chapter 2

16. According to the Abraham Lincoln Brigade Archives, Detro "was wounded by a sniper at Teruel on January 19, 1938 and died of complications in Murcia hospital on April 10, 1938."
17. Hochschild, "How Texaco Helped Franco Win the Spanish Civil War."
18. *Life*, July 1, 1940.
19. The photo caption actually states that the "Motilone Indian" boy was injured in a "fight" between Texaco employees and the indigenous inhabitants of the region, and the Texaco workers "adopted" the child and made him their "mascot."

Chapter 3

20. The miser and chief antagonist of *It's A Wonderful Life*.
21. "Murder Defense: Escort's Shooting Was Legal."
22. Texas Penal Code, Sec. 43.02. "PROSTITUTION. (a) A person commits an offense if the person knowingly offers or agrees to receive a fee from another to engage in sexual conduct."
23. Texas Penal Code, Sec. 9.42. "DEADLY FORCE TO PROTECT PROPERTY. A person is justified in using deadly force against another to protect land or tangible, movable property:
    (1) if he would be justified in using force against the other under Section 9.41; and
    (2) when and to the degree he reasonably believes the deadly force is immediately necessary:

(A) to prevent the other's imminent commission of arson, burglary, robbery, aggravated robbery, theft during the nighttime, or criminal mischief during the nighttime; or

(B) to prevent the other who is fleeing immediately after committing burglary, robbery, aggravated robbery, or theft during the nighttime from escaping with the property; and

(3) he reasonably believes that:

(A) the land or property cannot be protected or recovered by any other means; or

(B) the use of force other than deadly force to protect or recover the land or property would expose the actor or another to a substantial risk of death or serious bodily injury."

Acts 1973, 63rd Leg., p. 883, ch. 399, Sec. 1, eff. January 1, 1974. Amended by Acts 1993, 73rd Leg., ch. 900, Sec. 1.01, eff. September 1, 1994.

24. The abovethelaw.com headline read, "Killing a Hooker Is A-OK. Guess Which State," June 6, 2013.

25. "Killer Acquitted Under '73 Law; Man's Defense: Hired Escort Was a Thief, Stole $150.00."

26. "Murder Defense: Escort's Shooting Was Legal."

27. "Ezekiel Gilbert Acquitted of Murdering Woman Who Wouldn't Have Sex."

28. My San Antonio, "Man Accused in Shooting of Alleged Prostitute Back in Jail."

29. Ibid.

30. Murphy, "I-Team: Convicted Pimp Is Sentenced to Weekends in Jail."

Chapter 4

31. Once a thriving port on Matagorda Bay in Calhoun County, Indianola is now a ghost town. The community, originally the county seat of Calhoun County, is a part of the Victoria, Texas Metropolitan Statistical Area. In 1875, the city had a population of 5,000, but on September 15, 1875, a hurricane struck, killing between 150 and 300 residents and almost entirely destroying the town. Indianola was rebuilt, only to be wiped out again on August 19, 1886, by another hurricane, followed by a fire.

32. Weber, "Cart War," *Handbook of Texas.*

33. "An Atrocious and Damnable Deed," *State Gazette*, September 26, 1857.

34. It appeared in the *San Antonio Texan* on October 8, 1857.

NOTES TO PAGES 64–73

35. Lewis Cass (October 9, 1782–June 17, 1866) was an American military officer, politician and statesman. He represented Michigan in the United States Senate and served in the cabinets of two U.S. presidents, Andrew Jackson and James Buchanan. He was also the 1848 Democratic presidential nominee. A slave owner, Cass was one of the chief proponents for the doctrine of popular sovereignty, which held that the citizens of each territory should decide whether to permit slavery.
36. A native of Enfield, Connecticut, Elisha Marshall Pease (January 3, 1812–August 26, 1883) was the fifth and thirteenth governor of Texas.
37. The equivalent to over $500,000 today.
38. Lack, "Slavery and Vigilantism in Austin, Texas, 1840–1860," 4.
39. "Worthy of Notice."
40. Diaz, "To Carry That Burden."
41. *Texas Siftings*, an independent weekly, was started in Austin in May 1881 by Alexander E. Sweet and John Armoy Knox. The name of the publication was derived from a nom de plume, "Siftings," that Sweet used while he was a correspondent for the *Galveston Daily News* in San Antonio in 1878. When Sweet moved to Galveston in 1879 to become the editor of the *Daily News*, he ran a column, Galveston Siftings. Sweet left Galveston in December 1880 to move to Austin, where he bought the *Austin Weekly Review*, which he turned into *Texas Siftings*. The first edition of the publication appeared on May 9, 1881, and circulation quickly grew to 50,000 copies. In its first three years, *Texas Siftings* resembled a newspaper more than a magazine. Though it was established primarily as a humorous sheet, it contained some local and state news and editorials and, by 1885, had achieved a circulation of 100,000.
42. Interestingly enough, the Cart War created a transport shortage that left goods stranded and consumer demands unmet. In the end, members of the Know-Nothings who had previously condemned the Mexican American and Mexican "greasers" changed their minds and began to criticize the unprovoked molestations and murders the "greasers" suffered and lobbied for their protection and reenfranchisement.

Chapter 5

43. The headline of the story detailing the incident in the July 21, 1895 edition of the *Dallas Morning News*.

44. According to a manuscript from the Ohio Reading Road Trip, "By the mid-1800s, the streets of Northeastern cities were filled with poor children who were orphaned or whose parents could not take care of them. When groups like the New York Foundling Hospital and the Children's Aid Society offered to send these children to new homes in rural America, many desperate parents surrendered their sons and daughters in the hope that they would have a better life. The children were placed on trains (called 'Orphan Trains') and sent to their new homes. When the trains reached their destinations, people came to choose from the children on the train. Many children were adopted into loving homes, but others were abused by their foster parents or used as cheap labor on farms. Teenaged boys often ran away. Sometimes children were shuttled from foster home to foster home, ending up in different towns or even different states. Siblings were often separated, and some never found each other again. Nearly all of the children lost contact with their biological parents.

   "As they grew up, many of the Orphan Train children had mixed feelings about their experience. They were often sad or angry about being taken away from their parents, brothers, and sisters, or about the way they were treated by their foster families. Many Orphan Train riders recalled that the other people in the towns where they were placed were unfriendly or suspicious of them....The last Orphan Train left New York for Sulphur Springs, Texas, on May 31, 1929. In seventy-five years, between 100,000 and 250,000 children had been relocated across America." https://www.orrt.org/extensions/boundchildren.pdf.

45. Pioneering civil aviator Bessie Coleman, Ragtime legend Scott Joplin, blues legend Blind Lemon Jefferson, American labor organizer and Spanish Civil War military leader Oliver Law, to name a few.

46. Someone placed dynamite under a servant's quarters behind a Llano, Texas hotel in late July 1889 as well. The explosion blew them thirty feet, but they survived.

47. The Phillips residence was located on the Smith-Strange farm.

48. "That Terrible Explosion."

49. Ibid.

50. "Awful Revenge."

51. "That Terrible Explosion."

Chapter 6

52. Medina, "Overlooked No More: Jovita Idar, Who Promoted Rights of Mexican Americans and Women."

53. In a 1984 interview with Jerry Poyo and Tom Shelton for the Oral History Office of the Institute of Texan Culture.

54. Three died at birth, and one didn't survive childhood.

55. A designation connoting good, decent people living meaningful or productive lives.

56. From a 1984 interview with Jerry Poyo and Tom Shelton for the Oral History Office of the Institute of Texan Culture.

57. Originally known as the Laredo Seminary, the Holding Institute was founded in Laredo in 1880 by the Methodist Episcopal Church, South. Its site, overlooking the Rio Grande south of Fort McIntosh, was donated by Elias Robertson. Two Methodist ministers, A.H. Sutherland and Joseph Norwood, created the school for the instruction of Mexican children. In 1883, Nannie Emory Holding of Covington, Kentucky, arrived at the seminary and was its superintendent until 1913. During her administration, the school was enlarged to include seven buildings on a campus of twenty-six acres. A fifty-year charter was secured in April 1891. Bachelor's degrees in teacher training were awarded until 1913.

58. In 1928, thirty-five years before he became the president of the United States, LBJ spent a year teaching at what was known as the time as a "Mexican school." The conditions were abhorrent and left an indelible impression on him. On January 2, 1968, LBJ signed into law the first Bilingual Education Act, saying, "The bill contains a special provision establishing bilingual education programs for children whose first language is not English. Thousands of children of Latin descent, young Indians and others will get a better start."

59. Historian Albert M. Camarillo and others use the term *Jaime Crow*.

60. Women and young people. She also founded and ran *El Estudiante*.

61. A participant in the Mexican Revolution, Manuel García Vigil was born in Oaxaca on July 24, 1882. He was the governor of the state of Oaxaca from 1920 until 1923, but his support for the Delahuertista Rebellion led to his execution in San Jerónimo (now Ciudad Ixtepec), Oaxaca, on April 19, 1924. A statue of Vigil stands in the city of Oaxaca today.

62. The seven-month U.S. occupation of Veracruz (April 21–November 23, 1914) began with the Battle of Veracruz. The incident came in the midst

of poor diplomatic relations between the United States and Mexico and was related to the ongoing Mexican Revolution.

63. According to *Bad Mexicans: Race, Empire & Revolution in the Borderlands*, by Kelly Lytle Hernández (director of the Ralph J. Bunche Center for African American Studies and holder the Thomas E. Lifka Endowed Chair in History at UCLA), a similar circumstance occurred ten years earlier, except in that case, Mexican secretary of foreign affairs Ignacio Mariscal told the Mexican ambassador in Washington, D.C., to let the U.S. secretary of state know that Laredoan journalists were involved in "punishable acts" by trying to "disrupt public order in Mexico." Mariscal further insisted that their "machinations" should be thwarted by arrests.

64. The Spanish expression *La Raza* has historically been used to refer to the Hispanophone populations (mostly residing in the Western Hemisphere) considered as an ethnic or racial unit deriving from the Spanish empire and the process of racial intermixing of the Spanish colonizers with the indigenous populations of the Americas.

Chapter 7

65. Fort Stockton native Walter Buenger, PhD, is currently the Texas State Historical Association's chief historian.

Chapter 8

66. "Actor's Life Told in Novel."

67. Harris would appear as a "disaffected" youth in *The Inheritors* and then conclude his motion picture career with a role in *When Are You Coming Back, Red Ryder?*, a 1979 film (based on a Mark Medoff play) that also revolved around another strain of "disaffected" youth, this one of the Vietnam veteran variety (and played by Marjoe Gortner). On a personal note, I actually enrolled to complete my postgraduate work at New Mexico State University in the mid-1990s to study under (or in the vicinity of) Medoff. I wound up enrolling at the University of Texas at Arlington instead.

68. Scout badges are worn on the uniforms of members of youth Scouting organizations to signify membership and achievements.

69. I love this phrase. I took it to mean the hangover set.

70. The reviewer Anderson didn't seem to care for Lady Brett Ashley of Hemingway's *The Sun Also Rises* (1926), but many today consider Brett a strong, independent woman, even if she uses her sexual objectification as a means of exerting power over men. Interestingly, Anderson gave a glowing review of Ayn Rand's *The Fountainhead* (1943), whose main female character is also a strong, independent woman.
71. Presumably a play on words involving the popular 1924 book title *The Green Hat* (Iris March Edition), by Michael Arlen.
72. *Studs Lonigan* is a novel trilogy by American author James T. Farrell: *Young Lonigan*, *The Young Manhood of Studs Lonigan* and *Judgment Day*. In 1998, the Modern Library ranked the *Studs Lonigan* trilogy twenty-ninth on its list of the one hundred best English-language novels of the twentieth century.
73. Kaufman, "Rich Anthology of Southwest Assembled by George S. Perry."
74. It appeared in book form and also in *Texas Monthly* in August 1981 and May 2002.
75. Phillips, *Night Watch*.
76. "Attlee Is Relative of Mrs. Edwin T. Phillips."
77. Matt Krause was unsuccessful in his bid for the Tarrant County District Attorney's Office.

Chapter 9

78. Levenson, "Fort Hood Soldier Found Dead After Telling Family about Sexual Harassment."
79. Clips of this movie are used to great effect in the video for Metallica's song "One."
80. Katherine Anne Couric (born January 7, 1957) is an American journalist and presenter. In her early days, Couric was an assignment editor for CNN. Later, she was a television host at all of the U.S. "big three" television networks. She worked for NBC News from 1989 to 2006, CBS News from 2006 to 2011 and ABC News from 2011 to 2014. Couric was the cohost of *Today* and anchor of the *CBS Evening News* and a correspondent for *60 Minutes*. She is founder of Katie Couric Media, a multimedia news and production company. She also publishes a daily newsletter, *Wake Up Call*. In 2021, she appeared as a guest host for the game show *Jeopardy!*, the first woman to host the flagship American version of the show in its history. Couric's 2011 book, *The Best Advice I Ever Got: Lessons from Extraordinary*

Lives, was a *New York Times* bestseller. In 2004, Couric was inducted into the Television Hall of Fame.

81. Kingsville native Richard Edward Cavazos (January 31, 1929–October 29, 2017) was a U.S. Army four-star general. He was a Korean War recipient of the Distinguished Service Cross as a first lieutenant and advanced in rank to become the U.S. Army's first Hispanic four-star general. During the Vietnam War, as a lieutenant colonel, Cavazos was awarded a second Distinguished Service Cross. In 1976, he became the first Mexican American to reach the rank of brigadier general in the U.S. Army. Cavazos served for thirty-three years, with his final command as head of the United States Army Forces Command.

82. Afghanistan, Bahrain, Cuba (Guantanamo Bay), Cypress, Djibouti, Egypt, Eritrea, Ethiopia, Iraq, Israel, Jordan, Kenya, Kuwait, Kyrgyzstan, Lebanon, Oman, Qatar, Pakistan, Philippines, Saudi Arabia, Seychelles, Sudan, Syria, Tajikistan, Turkey, the United Arab Emirates, Uzbekistan and Yemen, etc.

83. Yes, it is an actual word. The non-slang definition is: no longer in working order and perhaps beyond repair.

84. Andone, "Here's What We Know About Eight of the Soldiers Who Have Died This Year at Fort Hood," Cnn.com, July 25, 2020.

85. Katy Forrester, "'Swept Under the Rug': Fort Hood Soldier Saw String of Sexual Assaults at Army Base Before He Died, Claims Widow," *U.S. Sun*, October 8, 2020.

86. Stillhouse Hollow Lake is a U.S. Army Corps of Engineers reservoir on the Lampasas River in the Brazos River basin, five miles southwest of Belton. The Stillhouse Hollow Dam and reservoir are managed by the Fort Worth District of the U.S. Army Corps of Engineers. The reservoir was officially impounded in 1968 and ensures flood control for the communities downstream. The reservoir is a popular recreation destination and serves as a water supply for several of the surrounding communities.

87. Meryosh, "14 Disciplined in Army Probe of Fort Hood." There was also a "Report of the Fort Hood Independent Review Committee" of the affair published (with some redactions): https://www.army.mil/e2/downloads/rv7/forthoodreview/2020-12-03_FHIRC_report_redacted.pdf.

88. Jeong, "'The Only Thing I Knew How to Do Was Kill People'."

89. White, "Skiatook Family's Son Dies on Fort Hood Military Base."

Chapter 10

90. The interview of whom is discussed in chapter 5 of *The 1910 Slocum Massacre: An Act of Genocide in East Texas* (2014).
91. *Ex Parte Spurger et al.* (Court of Criminal Appeals of Texas, May 10, 1911), 235.
92. Thomas Franklin Lee Hassell, 1863–1951.
93. The outrageous missive goes on and on, tracing the author's claims to the Bible. *Honey Grove Signal*, July 29, 1910.
94. Chapter 3 of *Texas Obscurities: Stories of the Peculiar, Exceptional and Nefarious* (2014).
95. *Black Holocaust: The Paris Horror and a Legacy of Texas Terror* (2015).
96. *Palestine Daily Herald*, June 21, 1910 (front page).
97. The first was titled *The First Eight*, and the narrative included Hollie-Jawaid's work in the present juxtaposed with the massacre itself in the past. The second screenplay was called *Ghosts of Slocum* and is available in book form.
98. *Ex Parte Spurger et al.*, 199.
99. Ibid., 175.
100. Ibid., 60–62.
101. Ibid., 252.

BIBLIOGRAPHY

Abilene Reporter-News. "Black Leaders Want Swift Action in Murder of Palestine Retiree." October 20, 1976.

———. "Gun Possibly Identified in Black Leader's Death." October 27, 1976.

———. "Police Chief Said No Sign of Intruder at Robinson Home." November 18, 1976.

Above the Law. "Killing a Hooker Is A-OK. Guess Which State." June 6, 2013. abovethelaw.com.

Amarillo Globe-Times. "Lawmakers Seek Probe into Death of East Texas Rights Leader." October 29, 1976.

Anderson, Bett. "Lost Youth." *Pittsburgh Press*, January 19, 1941.

Andone, Dakin. "Here's What We Know About Eight of the Soldiers Who Have Died this Year at Fort Hood." Cnn.com, July 25, 2020.

Arizona Daily Star (Tuscon, AZ), "Texas Mob Burns Negro to Death at Stake." January 21, 1919.

Atlanta Constitution. "Negro Is Burned in Public Square." January 21, 1919.

Austin American-Statesman. "Black Leader's Death Spurs Suicide Theory." October 21, 1976.

———. "Black Leader's Homicide Reported." October 14, 1976.

———. "'Conspiracy' Cited in Slaying." October 20, 1976.

———. "East Texas Death." October 27, 1976.

———. "Inquest Delay 'Possible'." October 28, 1976.

———. "Inquest Set Nov. 16 into Robinson Death." October 22, 1976.

———. "Plenty of Suspects If It Was a Murder." October 24, 1976.

———. "Ragsdale Wants FBI to Enter Slaying Probe." October 29, 1976.

———. "Robinson Files Subpoenaed." October 30, 1976.

———. "Visiting in the Library." November 28, 1943.

Austin Weekly Statesman. "Awful Revenge." July 25, 1895.

Bailey, Ellis. *A History of Hill County, Texas: 1838–1965.* Waco, TX: Texian Press, 1966.

Baltimore Sun. "The Inheritors." December 1, 1940.

Bills, E.R. *Black Holocaust: The Paris Horror and a Legacy of Texas Terror.* Fort Worth, TX: Eakin Press, 2015.

Birmingham (AL) News. "The Inheritors." January 5, 1941.

Brownsville Herald. "Blacks, Whites Differ on Death Cause." October 25, 1976.

Brownwood Bulletin. "Case of Hillsboro Lynchers Passed by Court of Appeals." March 12, 1919.

———. "East Texas Civil Rights Leader Shot with Own Gun." October 27, 1976.

———. "Inquest Jury Eyes Robinson Suicide." October 27, 1976.

———. "Police Ask for Help in Murder Case." October 15, 1976.

———. "Ranger Testifies No Burns Found on Victim." November 18, 1976.

Capshaw, Ron. "Doing Big Business with Fascists." *Tablet Magazine,* September 20, 2018.

Cashion, Ty. *The New Frontier: A Contemporary History of Fort Worth and Tarrant County.* San Antonio, TX: Historical Publishing Network, 2006.

Clifton Record. "Report Is Made on Hillsboro Lynching." February 28, 1919.

Colorado Citizen (Columbus, TX). "The Cart War Again." January 23, 1858.

Commerce Journal. "East Texas Race Riot: Several Are Killed." August 5, 1910.

Corpus Christi Caller. "Bragg Williams Negro, Burned at Hillsboro." January 21, 1919.

Corsicana Daily Sun. "Civil Rights Leader Probably Killed with His Own Shotgun." October 27, 1976.

———. "Hill Joins Murder Probe in Palestine." October 22, 1976.

———. "Negro Burned at Hillsboro." January 21, 1919.

———. "No Action on Motion." March 12, 1919.

———. "No Powder Burns on Robinson's Shirt." November 18, 1976.

Coronado, Acacia. "Another Soldier Reported Missing." *Brownsville Herald,* August 8, 2020.

———. "Ft. Hood Soldier Told of Abuse." *Philadelphia Inquirer,* August 27, 2020.

Crider, Bill. "Forgotten Books: *The Naked Year*—Philip Atlee." www.billcrider.blogspot.com.

Daily Courier (Connellsville, PA). "Not Race War; Just Slaughter." August 1, 1910.

Daily Kos. "Hey, Did You Hear the One About the Dead Hooker?" June 7, 2013.

Daily News Telegram (Sulphur Springs, TX). "Chief Supports Suicide Theory." October 26, 1976.

———. "Coroner's Jury Begins Probe." November 16, 1976.

Dallas Express. "Accused Was Sentenced to Hang February 21." January 25, 1919.

———. "The Growing Menace of Mobocracy." February 1, 1919.

———. "Hill County Grand Jury Fails to Return 'Lynching' Bills." July 19, 1919.

———. "Lynching Must Go." March 15, 1919.

Dallas Morning News. "Blown to Eternity." July 21, 1895.

———. "Death Leaves Puzzling Clues." October 24, 1976.

———. "Grand Jury Takes Up Investigation." August 2, 1910.

———. "Group Offers $2,000 Reward for Frank Robinson's Killer." November 21, 1976.

———. "Negro Is Burned to Death at Hillsboro." January 21, 1919.

———. "Officials Subpoena Robinson Records." November 3, 1976.

———. "Robinson Shot Himself, Jury Verdict Says." November 20, 1976.

———. "Seven Indictments in Anderson County." August 18, 1910.

———. "Woman's Club of TCU Gives Poetry Award." December 15, 1940.

Diaz, Maria. "To Carry That Burden." *Reconsidering Southern Labor History.* Gainesville: University Press of Florida, 2018, 63–77.

Eastern Texian (San Augustine, TX). "The Cart War." October 10, 1857.

Eichenwald, Kurt. "Why Ezekiel Gilbert's Acquittal Proves the Lunacy of Texas's Gun Laws." *Vanity Fair,* June 7, 2013.

Eyrich, Claire. "Author Selects the Best Texas Literature." *Fort Worth Star-Telegram,* October 8, 1982.

Fort Lauderdale News. "Rights Leader Shot Self, Police Think." October 26, 1976.

Fort Worth Gazette. "Result of Revenge." July 21, 1895.

Fort Worth Record. "Enraged Citizens Burn Negro Slayer." January 21, 1919.

Fort Worth Star-Telegram. "Attlee Is Relative of Mrs. Edwin T. Phillips." October 29, 1940.

———. "First Novel by Texan Has Fort Worth Scene." October 29, 1940.

———. "Fort Worth's Own Novel May Get Some Backs Up." October 29, 1940.

———. "Mob Lynches Negro Under Death Sentence." January 20, 1919.

———. "Ranger Testifies at Inquest." November 18, 1976.

———. "Victims of Slocum Mob Were Unarmed." August 1, 1910.

Galveston Daily News. "Colored People Excited." August 16, 1895.

———. "Condemned Negro Taken from Jail and Burned." January 21, 1919.

———. "Further Particulars." July 22, 1895.

———. "Gardner Delivered Grand Jury Charge." August 2, 1910, 9.

———. "That Terrible Explosion." August 5, 1895.

———. "Victims of Slocum Mob Were Unarmed." August 1, 1910.

———. "Whites and Blacks Clash, Eighteen Negroes Killed." July 31, 1910, 1.

Galveston Tribune. "A Frightful Crime." July 20, 1895.

Gamboa, Susan. "Ft. Hood to Officially Drop Its Confederate Name and Become Ft. Cavazos." NBC News, March 24, 2023. https://www.nbcnews.com.

Garza-Falcon, Leticia Magda. *Gente Decente: A Borderlands Response to the Rhetoric of Dominance.* Austin: University of Texas Press, 1998.

Gaudio, Lucy Del. "What Is Happening at Fort Hood?" Military.com, March 27, 2023.

George, Juliet. *Fort Worth's Arlington Heights.* Charleston, SC: The History Press, 2010.

Greene, A.C. "The Fifty Best Texas Books." *Texas Monthly*, August 1981.

Hanna, Bill. "James Phillips, 76, Wrote Novel of Fort Worth Society." *Fort Worth Star-Telegram*, May 27, 1991.

Harrison, Eric. "A Shadow of Doubt." *Fort Worth Star-Telegram*, June 20, 1982.

Hartford (CT) *Courant.* "Negro Burned to Death by Mob in Public Square." January 21, 1919.

Hernández, Kelly Lytle. *Bad Mexicans: Race, Empire & Revolution in the Borderlands.* New York: W.W. Norton & Company, 2022.

Hilley-Sierzchula, Emily. "Guilty: Fort Hood Veteran Sentenced to Life in Prison for Triple Murder." *Killeen Daily Herald*, March 31, 2022.

Hillsboro Mirror. "Bragg Williams Was Sentenced." January 22, 1919.

———. "Charge Given by Judge Horton B. Porter." January 29, 1919.

———. "A Dynamite Explosion." July 31, 1889.

———. "Negro Burned on Public Square." January 22, 1919.

Hochschild, Adam. "How Texaco Helped Franco Win the Spanish Civil War." *Time*, March 29, 2016.

———. *Spain in Our Hearts: Americans in the Spanish Civil War, 1936–1939*. New York: Houghton Mifflin Harcourt, 2016.

Houston Post. "Berry Starts New Process to Reach Mob Participants." February 27, 1919.

———. "Lynchers in Contempt?" February 23, 1919.

Huffington Post. "Ezekiel Gilbert Acquitted of Murdering Woman Who Wouldn't Have Sex." June 6, 2013.

Jaspin, Elliott. "Leave or Die: America's Hidden History of Racial Expulsions." *Austin American-Statesman*, July 9, 2006.

Jeong, Mae. "'The Only Thing I Knew How to Do Was Kill People': Inside the Rash of Unexplained Deaths at Fort Hood." *Vanity Fair*, July 6, 2021.

Jerreat, Jessica. "Texas Jury Acquit Man Who Shot Dead Craigslist Escort Who Refused to Have Sex with Him." Dailymail.com, June 6, 2013.

Juillerat, Maude F. "Crowd of Young Escapists." *Cincinnati Inquirer*, November 10, 1940.

Kaufman, Kenneth C. "Rich Anthology of Southwest Assembled by George S. Perry." *Chicago Tribune*, October 17, 1943.

Kirkus Reviews. "The Inheritors." June 15, 1940.

Lack, Paul D. "Slavery and Vigilantism in Austin, Texas, 1840–1860." *Southwestern Historical Quarterly* 85 (July 1981–April 1982).

Lampasas Leader. "Steps to End Mob Rule in Texas." January 24, 1919.

Lansing State Journal. "Actor's Life Told in Novel." February 16, 1941.

Lee, David. "Texas Escort Killer Acquitted of Murder." courthousenews. com, June 10, 2013.

Levenson, Michael. "Fort Hood Soldier Found Dead After Telling Family About Sexual Harassment." *New York Times*, March 17, 2023.

Longview Daily News. "Ranger Testifies in Death Probe." November 18, 1976.

Longview News Journal. "Help Requested in Murder Case." October 19. 1976.

Los Angeles Herald. "Murdered by Dynamite." July 21, 1895.

Lubbock Avalanche-Journal. "Assistant State Attorney Named to Investigation." October 22, 1976.

———. "Blacks Ask Aid in Death Probe." October 19, 1976.

———. "Inquest Underway in Shooting." November 18, 1976.

———. "Polygraph Shows Lie in Death Probe." November 19, 1976.

Madigan, Tim. "A Century Later, Race Massacre Forgotten by All but a Few." *Fort Worth Star-Telegram*, February 27, 2011.

———. "Story of Slocum Massacre of 1910 'Needs to Be Told'." *Fort Worth Star-Telegram*, March 6, 2011.

Mandia, Chris. "Man Acquitted of Killing Hooker Who Wouldn't Give Him Sex." Guns.com, June 7, 2013.

Manitoba (CAN) Free Press. "Negro, Sentenced to Hang, Burned at Stake in Texas." January 21, 1919.

McCabe, James D. *A Tour Around the World by General Grant: Being a Narrative of the Incidents and Events of His Journey.* Philadelphia: National Publishing Company, 1879.

McNeill, Maggie. "Rotten to the Core." *The Honest Courtesan* (blog), June 11, 2013. www.maggiemcneill.com.

Medina, Jennifer. "Overlooked No More: Jovita Idar, Who Promoted Rights of Mexican-Americans and Women." *New York Times*, August 7, 2020.

Merlan, Anna. "Sex Workers Pissed Off, Frightened by Acquittal of a San Antonio Man Who Killed an Escort." *Dallas Observer*, June 7, 2013.

Mervosh, Sarah. "14 Disciplined in Army Probe of Fort Hood." *Boston Globe*, December 9, 2020.

Michor, Max. "Two Accused of Recruiting Prostitute via Snapchat in Las Vegas." *Las Vegas Review-Journal*, September 22, 2017.

Mondo, Michelle, and Sam Peshek. "Jury Acquits Escort Shooter." mysanntonio.com, July 7, 2012.

Moravec, Eva Ruth. "Killer Acquitted Under '73 Law; Mann's Defense: Hired Escort Was a Thief, Stole $150.00." *San Antonio Express-News*, June 9, 2013.

Murphy, Vanessa. "I-Team: Convicted Pimp Is Sentenced to Weekends in Jail." KLAS, November 14, 2018. www8newsnow.com.

My San Antonio. "Man Accused in Shooting of Alleged Prostitute Back in Jail." June 7, 2013. www.mysanantonio.com.

NAACP. "An Appeal to the Conscience of the Civilized World." New York: NAACP, 1920.

———. "Burning at Stake in the United States." New York: NAACP, 1919.

Nebraska State Journal. "Burn Texas Negro to Death." January 21, 1919.

Nevins, Francis M. *Cornucopia of Crime: Memories and Summations.* Shreveport, LA: Ramble House, 2010.

Newspapers Artists' Association. *Makers of Fort Worth.* 1914.

New York Times. "Cavalry to Quell Outbreak in Texas." August 1, 1910.

———. "Philip Atlee, 77, Dies; Wrote Detective Novels." May 30, 1991.

———. "Score of Negroes Killed by Whites." July 31, 1910.

Odessa-American. "Civil Rights Leader's Death Cause Debated." November 17, 1976.

———. "Shotgun That Killed Robinson Identified as One He Owned." October 27, 1976.

Oliveira, Nelson. "It's Another Weird Death at Fort Hood." *New York Daily News*, September 5, 2020.

Palestine Daily Herald. "Frank Robinson Is Found Dead Here." October 14, 1976.

———. "Shooting Ruled Murder." October 15, 1976.

———. "Shotgun Apparently Belonged to Robinson." October 24, 1976.

Palo Pinto Star. "Untitled." July 18, 1885.

Paris Morning News. "Investigation of Hillsboro Mob Has Started in Austin." January 24, 1919.

———. "No Action Yet on Contempt Plea." February 22, 1919.

Paris News. "Help Is Sought to Solve Slaying." October 15, 1976.

Pennybacker, Anna J. Hardwicke. *A New History of Texas for Public Schools.* Palestine, TX: Percy V. Pennybaker, 1895.

Philadelphia Inquirer. "New 'Lost Generation'." February 19, 1941.

Phillips, David Atlee. *The Night Watch: 25 Years of Peculiar Service.* New York: Atheneum, 1977.

Powell, Dawn. "Scandal in the Cloakroom." *New Republic*, December 23, 1940.

Quiroga, Miguel Gonzalez. "Mexicanos in Texas during the Civil War." In *Mexican Americans in Texas History, Selected Essays*. Austin: Texas State Historical Association, 2000, 51–62.

Romero, Simon. "War of Words Divides Residents of Texas Town." *New York Times*, July 19, 2003.

San Antonio Evening News. "Atty General Brings Criminal Proceedings." February 20, 1919.

———. "Lynching Case Is Submitted to High Court." February 27, 1919.

San Antonio Express. "The Hill County Murderers." January 22, 1919.

———. "The Hillsboro Atrocity Investigated." January 25, 1919.

———. "Mob Law Condemned." February 4, 1919.

———. "Negro Is Spirited Away." December 5, 1918.

———. "$1,000 Reward." January 24, 1919.

———. "Steps to End Mob Rule in Texas Advocated in Legislature." January 23, 1919.

———. "Submit Motion in Contempt Case of Hill County Mob." February 27, 1919.

———. "Will Recommend New Legislation in His Message." January 22, 1919.

San Antonio Express-News. "Man Free on Bail in Shooting Case." December 29, 2009.

———. "Murder Defense: Escort's Shooting Was Legal." May 17, 2013.

San Antonio Texan. "The Mexican Cart War." September 24, 1857.

Sessions, Maxine. "Commissioner Rodney A. Howard, Sr. Tells History." *Cherokee County Informer* (Rusk, TX), January 1999.

Sherman Daily Democrat. "Negro Who Killed Woman and Child Is Burned." January 22, 1919.

Southwestern Reporter. *Ex Parte Spurger et al.* (Court of Criminal Appeals of Texas, May 10, 1911), 137, 351–54.

State of Texas vs. Bragg Williams Alias Snowball, Hill County Court Case No. 12810, 1919 (miscellaneous papers).

Tampa Bay (FL) *Times*. "Texas Mob Burns Negro Convicted of Murder." January 21, 1919.

Taylor, Lonn. "A Stealth Author from Fort Worth Is Revealed." *Big Bend Sentinel* (Marfa, TX), June 27, 2019.

Temple Daily Telegram. "Negroes Peeved at Mob at Hillsboro." January 23, 1919.

———. "Vindicates the Rangers." January 23, 1919.

Temple Times. "Negroes Killed with Dynamite." July 26, 1995.

Tennessean (Nashville, TN). "Mob Burns Nigger to Death." January 21, 1919.

Texas State Gazette (Austin, TX). "Worthy of Notice." February 24, 1855.

Thayer, Rose L. "'I Forgive You,' Mother of Slain Fort Hood Soldier Tells Man Convicted for His Killing." *Stars and Stripes*, April 1, 2022.

Thorndike, Joseph J., Jr. "'Cap' Rieber." *Life*, July 1, 1940.

Tyler Leader. "ET Police Chief Say Death Possible Suicide." October 28, 1976.

Vernon Record. "Legal Delay and Mob Law." January 24, 1919.

Waco News-Tribune. "Hillsboro Mob Burns Negro at City's Square." January 21, 1919.

———. "Negro Laughs as Jury Gives Death Sentence." January 18, 1919.

———. "Winchesters at Hillsboro Are Guarding Negro." January 17, 1919.

Washington Herald (Washington, D.C.). "Mob Seizes Murderer of Woman and Infant, Burns Him at Stake." January 21, 1919.

Weber, David J. "Cart War." *Handbook of Texas*, October 8, 2020. Texas State Historical Association. https://www.tshaonline.org.

Weekly Independent (Belton, TX). "Cart War." September 26, 1857.

———. "Untitled." December 5, 1857.

Weekly Telegraph (Houston, TX). "The Cart War Is Not Over." September 30, 1857.

White, Michele. "Skiatook Family's Son Dies on Fort Hood Military Base." FOX23, January 2, 2023.

White, Norris. "Palestine Man Led Fight for Civil Rights in East Texas." *Palestine Herald*, February 22, 2018.

Wichita Falls Times. "Brief Looks at New Books." February 23, 1941.

ABOUT THE AUTHOR

E.R. Bills is an award-winning author and freelance journalist. His works include *Texas Obscurities: Stories of the Peculiar, Exceptional and Nefarious* (2013), *The 1910 Slocum Massacre: An Act of Genocide in East Texas* (2014), *Black Holocaust: The Paris Horror and a Legacy of Texas Terror* (2015), *Texas Far and Wide: The Tornado with Eyes, Gettysburg's Last Casualty, the Celestial Skipping Stone and Other Tales* (2017), *The San Marcos 10: An Anti-War Protest in Texas* (2019), *Texas Oblivion: Mysterious Disappearances, Escapes and Cover-Ups* (2021), *Fear and Loathing in the Lone Star State* (2021) and *100 Things to Do in Texas Before You Die* (2022).

Bills has also written for the *Austin American-Statesman*, the *Fort Worth Star-Telegram*, *Texas Co-Op Power* magazine, *Fort Worth Magazine* and *Fort Worth Weekly*. He currently lives in North Texas with his wife, Stacie.

Visit us at
www.historypress.com